KOSHER CREOLE COOKBOOK

KOSHER CREOLE COOKBOOK

By Mildred L. Covert
and Sylvia P. Gerson

Illustrations by Alan Gerson

PELICAN PUBLISHING COMPANY
GRETNA 1982

Library of Congress Cataloging in Publication Data

Covert, Mildred L.
　Kosher Creole cookbook.

　Includes index.
　1. Cookery, Creole. 2. Cookery, American —
Louisiana. 3. Cookery, Jewish. I. Gerson,
Sylvia P. II. Gerson, Alan. III. Title.
TX715.C8675　　641.5'676　　81-15841
ISBN 0-88289-295-9　　　AACR2

Manufactured in the United States of America

Published by Pelican Publishing Company
1101 Monroe Street, Gretna, Louisiana 70053

*To our husbands, Lester and Dave,
who inspired us to become Kosher Creole cooks.*

Contents

Foreword

What does kosher mean? The root of this Hebrew word means "properly prepared." When used in connection with food, kosher has come to mean "ritually proper." It does not describe a kind of menu, cuisine, or style of cooking. Kosher food fulfills the requirements of the dietary laws enumerated in Leviticus 11.

The Bible repeats the verse "Thou shalt not seethe a kid in its mother's milk" three times (Exod. 23:14, 34:26, and Deut. 14:210). The age-old Hebrew practice of separating milk products from meat products arises from this biblical injunction. This system of separation dictates that no meat or foods containing meat or its by-products be cooked, prepared, served, or eaten with milk or foods containing milk or its by-products.

Food that is neither meat nor milk is often called "pareve" (neutral) and can be eaten at any time with any meal. All vegetables as well as pure vegetable and mineral products are considered pareve. Types of fish specified in Leviticus and eggs from the fowl listed in this section of the Bible are also considered pareve and can be enjoyed at all meals.

Many reasons are advanced for observing the dietary rules of Judaism. Traditionalists believe that these laws were divinely ordained to help keep us a holy people. Others add that practicing the restrictions is hygienically wise. There are those who stress the spiritual value of the discipline involved, while some modernists maintain that the laws should be observed in order to perpetuate Jewish identity.

Instilling holiness as a regulating principle—not simply an abstract ideal—in our daily lives remains the primary reason for adherence to the laws. They train us in the mastery of our appetites; they accustom us to restraining the growth of desire and the disposition to consider the pleasure of eating and drinking the end of man's existence. However, all would no doubt agree that the laws of kashruth have also been a significant factor in forming the unique character of the Jewish home. By means of these rules, religion enters the kitchen and accompanies the family to the table, designating it an altar of G-d.

Regarding the consumption of fish, Leviticus states "These shall ye eat of all that are in the water, whatsoever hath fins and scales" (Lev. 11:9). Thus shellfish, shrimp, lobster, crabs, turtles, eels, clams, and other scavenger fish cannot be eaten. Hence Creole cooking, which has many of the above as its basic ingredients, has heretofore been denied the kosher palate.

With great culinary skill and ingenuity, Sylvia Gerson and Mildred Covert—members of Congregation Beth Israel in New Orleans—have succeeded uniquely and creatively in making accessible the traditional flavors of Creole cooking while adhering completely to the laws of kashruth.

RABBI JONAH GEWIRTZ
Beth Israel Congregation
7000 Canal Boulevard
New Orleans, Louisiana

Preface

In the cultural and ethnic melting pot that is today's Louisiana, many traditions of yesterday are firmly and proudly preserved. Perhaps the most famous of these traditions is the art of Creole cooking—an art that commands respect throughout the culinary world.

Legend tells us that Creole cooking, indigenous to southern Louisiana, evolved through the skillful blending of French, Spanish, Negro, and Indian cooking, in recipes passed down through generations.

With the founding of Louisiana by Robert Cavelier, Sieur de La Salle in 1682, the French began to settle in the territory, bringing with them the culinary art of centuries of favorite Old-World dishes. In 1762 when Louisiana was ceded to Spain, the additional flavor of Spanish spices, aspics from the Aztecs, and condiments from the Caribbean, began to trickle into the bubbling cauldrons, emitting new aromas and creating delectable flavors. After the Louisiana Purchase of 1803, slaves—many of African origin and American-Indian descent—ruled the plantation kitchens and brought with them the herbs and seasonings of their respective tribes, adding yet another distinctive accent to the cuisine.

The development of the art of Creole cooking dates from colonial times in Louisiana. Kosher cooking dates back to the Bible, evolving from the observance of Jewish dietary laws (kashruth). The word "kosher" used in reference to food means ritually correct for consumption. The laws of kashruth prohibit the use of fish without fins and scales (e.g., catfish), shellfish and scavengers (shrimp, crab, lobster, oysters, clams), pork and its by-products (lard, bacon), and birds of prey. The combination of meat and dairy products is yet another dietary prohibition.

A reverence for the Jewish dietary laws as well as methods of preparing kosher dishes also have been handed down through generations. With the immigration of Sephardim (Mideastern) and Ashkenazim (Eastern-European) Jews to America, different versions of Jewish dishes also crossed the ocean. But regardless of ancestry, the Jewish cook maintained her tradition, adhering to the restrictions placed upon her in Biblical times. Food served from her kitchen remained kosher.

The question arises: How is it possible to be a Kosher cook and a Creole cook at the same time, especially since many of the most famous Creole recipes include such basic ingredients as seafood and pork for seasoning, and involve the combination of milk and meat products?

It was these very prohibitions as well as the tantalizing aromas and tastes of Creole cooking that challenged the authors of this book. One adopted native of New Orleans, whose background is steeped in traditional Jewish cooking, and a third-generation native of the city, of the same rich culinary background, sought new combinations and substitutions that would capture the flavors of Creole dishes while retaining the standards of kashruth.

Creativity became the underlying factor that enabled us to improvise and skillfully combine ingredients of the exotic Creole food and the delectable Kosher food so that the blending of both created Kosher-Creole—a new culinary form.

New Orleans, a fun-loving city, is enjoyed by natives and tourists the year round. And so we have conveniently arranged recipes month by month not only for the Kosher cook, the Creole cook, and for those who may be restricted in their intake of pork, seafood, etc., but also the daring and adventurous cook. To add to your pleasure, we have included some interesting facts and fiction surrounding "America's most interesting city."

MILDRED L. COVERT
SYLVIA P. GERSON

KOSHER CREOLE COOKBOOK

September

September

Traditional Kosher Creole
Festive Dining

Does it seem strange to you that we begin our cuisine calendar with September? A simple explanation will remedy that. It is at this time of year that the Jewish people commemorate the creation of the world and man—the beginning of life, the beginning of the year (according to the Hebrew lunar calendar), and the beginning of many festive occasions.

Traditionally, the celebration of all Jewish holidays commences in the home with a holiday meal. Food has always been important to the Jewish family, not simply because we like to eat and enjoy, but because we consider food a gift from the Lord. Eating is something special; we consider our kitchen the heart of the home, our table an altar to G-d, and it is here that the atmosphere is set for holiday fêting.

If you are ready to celebrate with us, take out your pots, pans, and utensils. Line up the ingredients. Follow directions and begin the new year with a new taste by serving your guests a traditional Kosher Creole meal.

September

Traditional Kosher Creole "Yom Tov" (Holiday) Meal

I.

Wine, round hallah, sliced apple, and honey*

Stuffed Mirliton	Zucchini Napoleon
Chicken Okra Gumbo With	Brandied Louisiana Yams
Sausage	Confederate Bread Pudding
Asparagus Vinaigrette Salad	Honey Sauce
Yom Tov Poulet	

II.

Wine, round hallah, sliced apple, and honey*

Trout Appétit	Eggplant à la Bonnie
Remoulade Sauce	Kosher Cajun Dirty Rice
Mirliton Soup	Ambrosia à la Vin en Rose
Rosbif Juteaux	Taka Hallah
String Beans Almondine	Hallah Bread

*It is a traditional custom to begin this holiday meal with blessings over the following:

Wine:
Blessed art Thou, Lord our God, King of the universe,
who creates the fruit of the vine.
Hallah:
Blessed art Thou, Lod our God, King of the universe,
who brings forth bread from the earth.
Apple (dipped into honey):
May it be Thy will, Lod our God and God of our Fathers,
to renew unto us a good and sweet year.
Blessed art Thou, O Lord our God, King of the universe,
who creates the fruit of the tree.

STUFFED MIRLITONS

9½ oz. tuna fish, drained
3 mirlitons
1 onion, chopped
2 cloves garlic, chopped
1 tbsp. pareve margarine
¼ cup chopped parsley
¼ cup chopped celery
¼ cup chopped green
   pepper

1 shallot, chopped
½ tsp. thyme
1 bay leaf, minced
¾ cup bread crumbs
salt and pepper to taste
paprika (optional)

Boil mirlitons in water until tender. Remove and cool, then cut in half. Scoop out (being careful not to damage shells) and mash pulp.

Brown onions and garlic in margarine. Add parsley, celery, shallots, green pepper, thyme, and bay leaf. Add bread crumbs, salt, pepper, and pulp. Mix well. Fry about 5 to 10 minutes, stirring often. Add tuna, mix well, and fry additional 5 minutes.

Fill mirliton shells with stuffing. Place additional bread crumbs on top and sprinkle with paprika. Dot each shell with margarine. Bake for about 15 minutes in 350-degree oven until golden brown on top. Serves six.

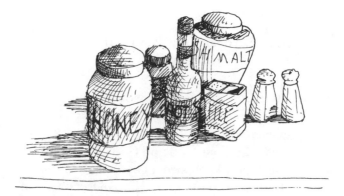

CHICKEN OKRA GUMBO WITH SAUSAGE

3 4-lb. chickens, cut up
½ cup vegetable oil
2 lbs. sliced okra
½ cup flour
1 gal. water
1 3-oz. kosher smoked
   sausage
1 lb. gizzards, cut up
2 medium onions, chopped
¼ bell pepper, chopped
1 whole bulb garlic,
   chopped

2 tbsp. chopped parsley
1 tbsp. sugar
1 6-oz. can tomato paste
3 large tomatoes or 1 16-oz.
   can whole tomatoes
2 bay leaves
pinch of thyme
1 tbsp. filé
salt and pepper to taste

Brown chicken pieces in some of the oil; remove from pot. Brown okra and remove from pot. Add remainder of oil and flour, stirring constantly until roux is a rich brown.

Add okra and water to roux, blending well. Add chicken, sausage, gizzards, and remaining ingredients except filé. Salt and pepper to taste. Cook for 1½ to 2 hours.

Stir in filé during the last ½ hour of cooking. Serve with cooked rice in soup bowls. Serves twelve to fifteen.

ASPARAGUS VINAIGRETTE SALAD

1 tsp. sugar
⅛ tsp. cayenne pepper
dash garlic juice
1 cup olive or salad oil
2 tbsp. chopped parsley
2 15-oz. cans whole
  asparagus, drained

1½ tsp. salt
¼ tsp. paprika
⅓ cup tarragon vinegar
¼ cup chopped shallots or
  onions
2 tbsp. chopped pimento
1 tbsp. capers

Combine sugar, salt, cayenne pepper, paprika, and garlic juice in a bowl. Add vinegar and oil slowly, beating constantly. Add onions or shallots, parsley, pimento, and capers; mix well. Pour over asparagus and refrigerate overnight. Serves four to six.

YOM TOV POULET

1 5- to 6-lb. pullet
1 cup concentrated tomato
  soup, undiluted
1½ cups boiling water
1 cup canned sliced
  mushrooms
liquid from mushrooms
½ cup chopped celery
1 rounded tbsp. pareve
  margarine

1 tbsp. flour
1 tbsp. chopped onion
1 tbsp. chopped green
  pepper
1 tbsp. chopped parsley
salt and pepper to taste
liquid vegetable shortening

Cut chicken into eight pieces. Season with salt and pepper and dredge with flour. Pour enough shortening into large skillet to cover bottom and heat to 375 degrees. Slowly brown chicken on both sides, keeping skillet covered. Remove and set aside.

In separate large saucepan, melt margarine; add onion and flour; brown lightly. Stir in tomato soup and water; mix well. Add parsley, green pepper, and celery. Bring to a rolling boil; add chicken. Lower flame and cook slowly about 1½ to 2 hours until chicken is tender.

Cook mushrooms in liquid for 15 minutes; add to chicken. Raise heat and bring mixture to boil once. Remove and serve. Serves six.

ZUCCHINI NAPOLEON

2 lbs. zucchini
¼ cup chopped onions
3 tbsp. pareve margarine
4 medium tomatoes, peeled
   and quartered

½ tsp. salt
¼ tsp. oregano
dash pepper
1 tbsp. flour (for Passover, substitute potato starch)

Cut zucchini into ½-inch slices. Sauté onions in margarine until tender. Add tomatoes and cook 5 minutes. Then add zucchini, salt, oregano, and pepper. Cook covered over low heat until zucchini is tender (about 12 to 15 minutes). If a thicker sauce is desired, sprinkle in flour and cook a few minutes longer. Serves six.

BRANDIED LOUISIANA YAMS

4 tbsp. pareve margarine
½ cup firmly packed brown
   sugar
1 tsp. grated orange peel
½ cup brandy

8 medium Louisiana yams, cooked, peeled, and sliced or 2 1-lb. cans Louisiana yams, drained and sliced

Melt margarine in large skillet. Add sugar and stir over low heat until melted. Add yams, orange peel, and brandy and cook over low heat 15 minutes, basting yams frequently. Serves eight.

CONFEDERATE BREAD PUDDING

6 to 8 slices stale bread
2 eggs
¼ cup sugar
½ cup seeded raisins
1 pt. nondairy creamer

1 pt. water
½ tsp. cinnamon
1 tsp. lemon extract
1 cup slightly salted water

Dip slices of stale bread in salted water until soft. Drain and place in a bowl, adding well-beaten eggs, sugar, and seeded raisins.

Scald nondairy creamer combined with water; add cinnamon and lemon extract and blend. Pour over bread and fill greased pudding dish with mixture.

Set in a pan of hot water and bake in 350-degree oven about 45 minutes. Serves six.

HONEY SAUCE

⅓ cup pareve margarine
3 egg yolks
1 tbsp. honey

1 cup sugar
⅓ cup boiling water

Cream margarine and sugar. Add slightly beaten egg yolks and water and cook over very low flame until mixture thickens. Remove from flame and add honey. Serve over bread pudding. Makes ½ cup.

TROUT APPÉTIT

1½ lbs. smoked trout (can
  be purchased at a kosher
  delicatessen)

Remove skin and bones from fish. Flake and place in cocktail glasses lined with lettuce leaves. Chill well. Spoon Remoulade Sauce (see recipe) on top just before serving. Serves four to six.

REMOULADE SAUCE

4 tbsp. horseradish
mustard
½ cup tarragon vinegar
2 tbsp. catsup
1 tbsp. paprika
½ tsp. cayenne pepper

1 tsp. salt
1 clove garlic
1 cup salad oil
½ cup shallots
½ cup chopped celery

Place ingredients in blender and blend thoroughly. Chill before serving.

MIRLITON SOUP

4 medium-size mirlitons
6 slices kosher Beef Frye
3 cloves garlic, chopped
1 large green pepper,
chopped
2 large onions, chopped
4 or 5 shallots, chopped
2 tbsp. chopped parsley
¼ tsp. oregano

1 bay leaf
5 chicken bouillon cubes
dissolved in 4 cups
boiling water
salt and pepper to taste
1 cup nondairy creamer
bread crumbs

Boil mirlitons until tender; let cool. Peel and cut into cubes. Set aside. In large pot fry Beef Frye until brown. Add all seasonings and sauté until soft. Add cubed mirlitons and chicken bouillon. Bring to a boil and cook for about 45 minutes.

Add nondairy creamer and simmer for 5 minutes. Then put soup in blender and blend until creamy. Serve hot with about 1 tablespoon bread crumbs on top. Serves six.

ROSBIF JUTEAUX

5½- to 6-lb. brisket,
  trimmed
1 ¾-oz. envelope kosher
  onion soup mix
garlic salt to taste

¼ tsp. pepper
½ cup water
1 tsp. salt

Place brisket fat side up in large baking or roasting pan. Bake for 10 minutes at 400°; then reduce heat to 350°. Sprinkle meat with soup mix, garlic, and seasonings and bake 15 minutes. Add water, cover pan, and reduce temperature to 325°. Bake 2 to 2½ hours or until meat can be pierced easily with a fork. Thicken drippings with a little flour and serve with brisket. Serves eight.

STRING BEANS ALMONDINE

1 lb. fresh string beans or
  1 16-oz. can French-style
  sliced string beans
¼ cup liquid from beans

½ stick pareve margarine
½ cup slivered almonds
¼ tsp. oregano
salt and pepper to taste

Wash fresh beans and remove ends and strings. Cover with boiling water to which ½ tsp. salt has been added. Cook uncovered for 20 to 30 minutes, or until tender. Drain and reserve ¼ cup liquid. Slice beans lengthwise into long, thin strips.

Melt margarine in saucepan. Add almonds and sauté until edges are light brown. Remove with slotted spoon. Add ¼ cup liquid from beans and stir. Add string beans and heat thoroughly, stirring occasionally. Add oregano and almonds; salt and pepper to taste and mix lightly with fork until heated through. Serves four.

EGGPLANT À LA BONNIE

4 eggplants
½ lb. pareve margarine
1 onion, chopped
3 cloves garlic
1 rib celery, finely chopped
1 tbsp. chopped parsley
¼ green pepper, finely
   chopped

pinch of thyme
salt and pepper to taste
½ lb. chopped kosher
   salami
1 lb. ground beef
4 eggs, well beaten
1 small loaf French bread

Boil eggplants in water until tender. Remove from pot, reserving water. Allow eggplant to cool. Scoop out pulp and set aside.

In the meantime, put margarine in large skillet and melt over medium flame. Add onions, garlic, celery, parsley, green pepper, and salami and sauté until golden brown. Lower the flame and add ground beef. Continue cooking, stirring occasionally to prevent sticking.

Take French bread and soften in reserved eggplant water, squeezing out excess liquid. Add softened bread to eggplant and stir in eggs. Add eggplant mixture to seasonings and continue cooking until ingredients are well done.

Remove from skillet and place in a well-greased 2-quart baking dish. Sprinkle with bread crumbs and paprika. Bake in 350-degree oven for 30 minutes. Serves twelve.

KOSHER CAJUN DIRTY RICE

2 cups uncooked long-
grain white rice
½ lb. cooked fresh
mushrooms, chopped or 1
4-oz. can chopped
mushrooms
liquid from mushrooms
½ cup chopped bell pepper
½ lb. kosher smoked
sausage

chopped parsley
2 onions, chopped
1½ sticks pareve margarine
1 cup chopped celery
3 chicken livers
3 chicken gizzards
2 cups clear chicken broth
1 cup water
pepper to taste

Boil gizzards until tender (about 30 to 35 minutes); broil livers until brown; and sauté sausage until slightly brown. Drain meats and dice.

Sauté onions in heavy iron skillet until light brown. Add bell pepper, celery, and mushrooms and cook until onions are transparent. Add remaining ingredients except sausage. Cover and cook on low heat 40 minutes, stirring often. Add sausage and place in 2-quart chafing dish. Garnish with parsley. Serves six.

AMBROSIA À LA VIN EN ROSÉ

4 grapefruit
1 pineapple
⅓ to ½ cup sugar
nutmeg

6 oranges
1 pt. strawberries
shredded coconut
½ cup white or rosé wine

Dice pineapple; cut grapefruit and oranges in sections. Wash berries and remove stems; add to fruits. Add sugar and let steep for several hours in refrigerator. Before serving, add wine. Sprinkle with shredded coconut and nutmeg. Serves six.

TAKA HALLAH

Make 2 days before Shabbas

2 tsp. salt
¼ cup oil
2 eggs, slightly beaten
½ cup sugar
pinch saffron
4 to 6 drops yellow food
   coloring

6 to 6½ cups sifted flour
2 pkgs. yeast
2 cups lukewarm water
½ cup white raisins
poppy seeds

In large mixer bowl, mix 1½ cups flour, sugar, salt, saffron, and yeast. Add oil all at once; gradually add water. Beat 2 minutes at medium speed of mixer. Add eggs, ½ cup flour, and food coloring. Beat at high speed 2 minutes. Stir in 2 cups flour, then remaining 2¼ cups. Pat dough and sides of bowl with a little oil. Cover with moist towel and refrigerate at least 24 hours.

The next day: punch down and let rise again in refrigerator 12 to 24 hours.

The next day: flour board; divide dough into 4 pieces. Press raisins into each section of dough using kneading motion. Divide each loaf into 4 pieces (total 16 pieces). Roll pieces about 1 inch thick and about 8 to 10 inches long. Pinch 3 pieces together at end and braid; pinch other end. Place fourth piece on top of braid and pinch ends. (For Yom-tov form a round braided loaf.)

Let stand, covered with dry towel, at room temperature for 1 hour. Brush with slightly beaten egg and sprinkle with poppy seeds. Bake at 400° for 20 to 25 minutes. Makes four loaves.

HALLAH BREAD

2¼ cups warm water
1 pkg. active dry yeast
2 tbsp. sugar
1 tbsp. salt
¼ cup peanut oil
pinch saffron
poppy seeds

2 eggs, beaten
8 cups unsifted flour
1 egg yolk
1 tbsp. water
½ cup raisins
4 drops yellow food coloring

Measure warm water into a large bowl that has been warmed in the oven. Sprinkle in yeast and stir until dissolved. Stir in sugar, salt, saffron, oil, eggs, and 4 cups of flour; beat until smooth. Add enough additional flour to make a soft dough. Turn out onto lightly floured board. Knead until smooth and elastic. Add raisins and continue kneading about 10 minutes. Place in oiled bowl, turning to grease top. Cover; let rise in a warm place, free from draft, until doubled in bulk (about 1 hour).

Punch down dough; turn out on lightly floured board and divide into 8 pieces. Shape each piece into a 14-inch strand and braid 3 of these strands together. Make a shallow depression down the center of the braid. Place a fourth strip of dough in this depression, stretching the strip the length of braid. Tuck ends of strip underneath braid and place on oiled baking sheets. Cover; let rise in warm place, free from draft, until doubled (about 45 minutes).

Combine egg yolk and water; brush tops of braids, sprinkle with poppy seeds. Bake at 350° for 30 minutes or until done. Makes two large loaves.

October

October
Brewings from the Bayou

The lilting phrase "down on the bayou" conjures up visions of muddy waters from the Mississippi, sluggishly drifting inland, creating the mysterious swamps, marshes, and small streams that line the banks of Louisiana's lowlands. Beautiful yet forbidding, bayou country is like another world.

The notorious pirate Jean Lafitte and his buccaneers once lived in this semitropical wilderness. It was here in the maze of bayous in the Barataria region not far from New Orleans that his band of pirates hid out.

The bayou is also home to the French-speaking Cajuns. Immortalized in Henry Wadsworth Longfellow's *Evangeline, A Tale of Acadia* (1847), the former Acadians—ousted from Nova Scotia because of their religious beliefs—settled in southeastern Louisiana. Unable to pronounce the word "Acadian," Indians in the region shortened it to Cajun. Many descendants of the Acadians live on houseboats as their forebears did more than a hundred years ago and continue to make their livelihoods hunting, trapping, and fishing in the bayou.

The Cajuns, by using their own variety of spices, added much to Creole cooking. They still provide us with their catches from the bayous, as well as red, green, and yellow peppers, thyme, mint, basil, sassafras (from which filé is made), pecans, mirlitons (a vine-grown, pear-shaped vegetable of the gourd family, similar to squash), okra, yams, sugarcane, and rice—all mainstays of Kosher Creole dishes.

As the Cajun skiff glides in and out of the shallow passes, the boulevards of Cajun country, life takes on a slow, easy pace. There is time to relax, gaze on the beauty of nature, think, and reminisce. And what better way to end the day than with a leisurely repast made from brewings from the bayou?

KOSHER CREOLE COOKBOOK

October

I.

Bak-o-Bayou Salad
Pirogue Onion Soup
Bayou Baked Red Snapper
Corn Fritters
Creole Okra and Tomatoes
French Bread
Rice Pudding
Café au Lait

II.

Mock Crawfish Salad
Redfish Courtbouillon
Eggplant in Batter
Buccaneer Fluffy Rice
Garlic Bread
Lafitte Caramel Custard
"By-You" Coffee

BAK-O-BAYOU SALAD

1 head iceberg lettuce
1 bunch watercress
2 creole tomatoes, cut into
  wedges
1 medium onion, sliced
½ clove garlic, crushed

½ cup mayonnaise
1½ tbsp. anchovy paste
1½ tbsp. tarragon vinegar
1½ tsp. lemon juice
3 tbsp. chopped parsley
pareve imitation bacon bits

Tear lettuce into large pieces and cut watercress into small pieces. Place lettuce, watercress, and tomatoes in a bowl. Separate onion slices into rings and add to lettuce mixture. Chill.

Blend garlic with mayonnaise and anchovy paste in a bowl, then stir in vinegar and lemon juice slowly. Add parsley and chill.

Pour dressing over lettuce mixture and garnish with imitation bacon bits. Serves six.

PIROGUE ONION SOUP

3 tbsp. butter
5 medium onions, sliced
  thin
6 cups pareve bouillon
½ tsp. salt
½ cup Sauterne wine

⅛ tsp. cayenne pepper
⅛ tsp. pepper
toast rounds
¼ cup grated Swiss or
  Meunster cheese

Melt 3 tablespoons butter in a large saucepan. Add onions and cook, stirring frequently, until golden brown. Add wine and cook additional 5 minutes. Add bouillon, salt, cayenne pepper, and pepper and bring to a boil. Cover and simmer for 15 minutes.

Pour into 6 soup bowls and place toast rounds in each. Sprinkle with grated cheese and serve. Serves six.

BAYOU BAKED RED SNAPPER

1 4-lb. whole red snapper
1 stick butter or pareve
  margarine
1 bunch shallots, chopped
½ tsp. oregano

1 11½-oz. can button
  mushrooms or 8 large
  fresh mushrooms
salt and pepper to taste

Clean fish and pat dry. Rub cavity with salt, pepper, and margarine. Place in well-greased baking pan and set aside.

Heat 3 or 4 tbsp. margarine in heavy skillet. Add shallots and sauté until soft, but not brown. Add more margarine and mushrooms and continue cooking, shaking pan until most of fat is absorbed. Stir in oregano and pour mixture over fish. Measure fish at its thickest point and bake exactly 10 minutes per inch of thickness in preheated 450-degree oven. Baste several times with pan juices. Serves eight to ten.

CORN FRITTERS

2 cups cooked white corn
1 tsp. salt
⅛ tsp. pepper
2 eggs, separated

1 tsp. melted butter
½ cup milk
2 cups flour
2 tsp. baking powder

Chop corn fine. Add salt, pepper, beaten egg yolks, butter, milk, flour, and baking powder. Mix well. Beat egg whites until stiff. Fold gently but thoroughly into batter.

Heat oil in deep fryer or heavy skillet to 360°. Drop batter by tablespoon into fat, allowing room for expansion. (Fritters will swell and surface quickly.) Fry 2 to 3 minutes, or until brown on both sides, turning only once. Remove fritters and drain on absorbent paper. Makes about one dozen.

(When serving with meat dishes, substitute ¼ cup water together with ¼ cup nondairy creamer for milk, and use schmaltz or pareve margarine in place of butter.)

CREOLE OKRA AND TOMATOES

½ cup pareve margarine
1 large onion, minced
½ bell pepper, diced
1 qt. sliced okra

4 fresh tomatoes, coarsely
    chopped
salt and pepper to taste

Melt margarine in large skillet or heavy pot; add onion and sauté over medium heat until transparent. Add bell pepper, okra, and tomatoes and season to taste. Lower heat, cover, and simmer 20 minutes. Stir occasionally. Serves eight to ten.

FRENCH BREAD

1 pkg. yeast
2 tsp. salt
1 tbsp. sugar
¼ cup yellow cornmeal

1¼ cups warm water
1 tbsp. shortening
3½ cups sifted flour

Dissolve yeast in water. Add salt, shortening, and sugar; stir in flour. Knead on lightly floured board until smooth. Place in greased bowl; brush lightly with additional shortening. Cover. Let rise in warm place until doubled in bulk (about 30 minutes). Punch down and divide into 2 equal portions. Roll each half into an oblong 15- by 10-inch roll. Roll up tightly beginning at the wide end. Seal ends by pinching together. Roll dough back and forth to taper ends; place shaped loaves, fold down, on greased baking sheets. Sprinkle loaves with cornmeal and brush with Cornstarch Glaze (see recipe).

Let rise, uncovered, until almost doubled in bulk (about 1 to 1½ hours). Brush again with Cornstarch Glaze. Make ¼-inch slashes in dough at 2-inch intervals. Place large pan of boiling water on lower rack of oven; place bread on rack above and bake in 400-degree oven 10 minutes. Remove from oven and brush again with glaze. Continue baking 30 minutes or until brown. Makes two loaves.

Cornstarch Glaze

1 tsp. cornstarch
½ cup boiling water
1 tsp. cold water

Combine cornstarch and cold water. Gradually add boiling water and cook until smooth. Cool slightly.

RICE PUDDING

1 cup uncooked rice
2 cups water
½ cup white raisins
2 tbsp. sugar
1 tbsp. butter
½ tsp. salt
1 cup milk
½ cup confectioners' sugar

2 eggs
½ cup drained crushed
   pineapple
1 tbsp. grated orange rind
⅔ cup red currant jelly
½ cup chopped pecans
¼ tsp. vanilla extract

Combine rice, water, raisins, sugar, butter, and salt in a 3-quart saucepan. Bring to a boil. Stir; cover and simmer for 15 minutes.

While mixture cooks, make a custard by beating together the confectioners' sugar and eggs. Scald milk, gradually stir into egg mixture, and return to pan. Cook over low heat, stirring constantly, until mixture thickens. Fold in rice mixture. Add crushed pineapple, orange rind, and vanilla. Mix well. Spoon into 1½-quart mold or 6 individual custard cups. Cool slightly. Heat jelly in small saucepan until melted. Unmold and serve with melted jelly and pecans. Serves six.

CAFÉ AU LAIT

3 cups strong, hot coffee
3 cups boiling milk
sugar to taste

Pour boiling milk and hot coffee simultaneously into serving cups. Sweeten to taste. Serves six.

MOCK CRAWFISH SALAD

3 lbs. red snapper fillets
4 slices lemon
1 small onion, sliced
1 cup celery, chopped fine
1 large carrot, grated
2 qts. water

1 minced onion or 2 tbsp.
instant minced onion
¾ cup chili sauce
1 cup mayonnaise
2 tsp. salt
¼ tsp. pepper

Bring water to boil in large kettle. Add red snapper, lemon, sliced onion, salt, and pepper. Continue to boil for 20 minutes. Drain fish; cool and flake.

Toss fish with minced onion, celery, carrot, chili sauce, and mayonnaise. Adjust salt and pepper to taste. Chill overnight. Serves eight to ten.

REDFISH COURTBOUILLON

1 5- to 6-lb. whole redfish
½ cup salad oil
¾ cup flour
2 large onions, finely
    chopped
4 shallots, chopped
2 cloves garlic, finely
    chopped
2 green peppers, chopped
2½ cups canned whole
    tomatoes

2 bay leaves
2 sprigs thyme, chopped
2 ribs celery, chopped
2 tbsp. chopped parsley
1¼ cups water
dash hot pepper sauce
salt and pepper to taste
lemon slices
pimento strips
parsley sprigs

Scale and gut fish; rinse well and pat dry. Make roux with salad oil and flour; add onions and shallots and brown. Add garlic, green peppers, tomatoes, bay leaves, thyme, celery, parsley, water, hot pepper sauce, salt, and pepper. Simmer in heavy iron skillet for about 1 hour. Place fish in rectangular Pyrex baking dish or roasting pan. Pour mixture over fish and bake in 350-degree oven for 45 minutes, or until fish is tender when tested with fork. Remove bay leaves before serving. Garnish with lemon slices studded with pimento strips and parsley sprigs. Serve with fluffy white rice. Serves six to eight.

EGGPLANT IN BATTER

1 cup flour
½ tsp. salt
dash pepper
⅔ cup milk or nondairy
    creamer

2 eggs, beaten
1 eggplant, cut into slices or
    chunks
4 tbsp. vegetable shortening

Sift dry ingredients together. Combine milk or nondairy creamer and eggs; beat into dry mixture. Dip eggplant into batter and fry in shortening at 375° until golden brown. Drain. Serves six.

BUCCANEER FLUFFY RICE

1 cup white long-grain rice
3 qts. water
1 tbsp. salt

Wash rice; drop it into salted boiling water and boil rapidly, uncovered, for 15 to 20 minutes or until kernels are soft when pressed between thumb and finger. Place in a colander and pour boiling water over rice to remove loose starch and separate grains.

Drain well. (Grains should be fluffy and separate.) Serves six.

GARLIC BREAD

1 loaf French bread
4 large cloves garlic,
   chopped very fine

2 sticks butter or pareve
   margarine
½ bunch parsley

Heat butter or margarine and garlic. Let stand. When ready to serve, pour garlic butter over bread, and sprinkle with parsley. Place in oven to heat.

LAFITTE CARAMEL CUSTARD

3 cups milk
⅓ cup sugar
½ tsp. lemon extract
3 eggs

2 tbsp. sugar
1 tbsp. hot water
tiny pinch salt
grated nutmeg (optional)

Scald milk. Put sugar in skillet and let melt to brown liquid. Add hot water gradually, stirring until free of lumps, then pour into hot milk.

Beat eggs slightly and add milk mixture gradually, stirring constantly. Add balance of sugar, salt, and extract.

Strain into buttered custard cups or pudding dish. Heat oven to 400°. Pour enough hot water into bottom of roasting pan to measure about ½ inch. Place custard cups in pan and bake for 20 minutes or until set. (When steel knife is inserted in center of custard and it comes out clean, custard is set.) Remove from pan. Allow to cool, and chill in refrigerator 1 hour or until ready to serve. Grated nutmeg may be sprinkled on top if desired. Serves six.

"BY-YOU" COFFEE

8 to 16 tbsp. drip-grind chicory coffee

**4 cups water
sugar to taste**

Fill a drip coffee maker with boiling water, then drain. Place coffee in filter section of coffee maker. Pour water into a saucepan and bring to a boil.

Pour 2 tablespoons water over coffee and let it drip through. Repeat small additions of boiling water 5 times. Place coffee maker over very low heat and repeat additions until all water is used. Do not let coffee boil. Remove filter section and stir coffee. Cover and serve. Serves four.

November

November

Vieux Carré Voodoos ("Voo-den")

The Vieux Carré, which means "old square," is an area of approximately 260 acres or about 90 square blocks located in downtown New Orleans. It is often referred to as the French Quarter. Here in 1722, boundaries were laid out for the city designated to be the capital of France's new-found American empire. Today the Vieux Carré is a city within a city, one that continues to retain its European heritage. Here one almost senses that another era of history has stood still and is ignoring the hustle and bustle of today's world.

A walking tour is a must when visiting the French Quarter. The architecture, reflecting the influence of three ruling nations (France, Spain, and America) has been carefully preserved. In fact, each street bears its name in three different languages in recognition of the contribution made by each nation. From the street you can see beautiful iron-laced balconies or secluded patios enclosed by a wrought-iron gate; and there is a visible lack of steps leading into entrances. In the early years, the city fathers, seeking revenues, heavily taxed not only steps, but chimneys as well. After the Louisiana Purchase in 1803, the enterprising Americans built stores on the ground floor, bringing additional commerce to the Quarter.

The Pontalba Apartments, completed in 1850, are believed to be the first apartment buildings in America. The cast iron grillwork with the cartouche of A & P (the initials standing for Almonester, Madame Pontalba's maiden name, and Pontalba, her married name) was introduced with the construction of this building. Today it houses luxury apartments and commercial shops. A few blocks beyond the Pontalba Apartments is Madame La Laurie's haunted house, where she allegedly chained and beat her slaves nightly. Years later, tenants continued to report the nightly howlings of the mistreated slaves. Still more colorful tales emerge with a visit to Congo Square, where slaves and free men of color were allowed to congregate on Sunday evenings. They brought with them the practice of voodoo. The Square was the scene of such dances as the "calinda"—a sensuous African dance where men and women faced each other. Participants also danced the "bamboula" to the beat of a drum made of bamboo.

In the early 1800s the devotees of voodoo worshiped a snake in secret rites concluding with frenzied dancing. Marie Laveau, best known of the voodoo queens, was a hairdresser. She became a power among the superstitious members of her race and many white people, who sought her advice as well as the gris-gris (pronounced gree-gree) she sold. These were charms or amulets for good or evil. Many were concoctions of salt, gunpowder, saffron, and dried dog dung. Gris-gris balls as large as oranges were made from brightly colored feathers. Some gris-gris were secreted in a pillow or a bed. Others, such as a cross of wet salt, were placed on the doorstep and meant trouble for the recipient; a small coffin on the gallery meant death. A favorite good luck gris-gris was a dime with a hole in it, worn around the ankle. There were love potions, money-making incense, "boss-fixing" potions, the black candle, and the famous pin-ridden voodoo doll.

The Voodoo cult continues to exist today. Whether fact or fiction, mysticism and tales surrounding voodooism still abound, fascinating natives and visitors alike.

There is no mysticism surrounding the following recipes. Rather, the directions are concise, the herbs and spices abundant; together they will be as stimulating to your taste buds as were the ritual dances to the devotees of voodooism.

November

I.

Broiled Grapefruit Laveau
Eggs Bene-Lox
Hollandaise Sauce
Fried Grits
Creole-Style Tomatoes
Sabra Crepes
Café Brûlot

II.

Gallery Biscuits
Vieux Carré Spinach Salad
Voo-den Veal Grillades
Gris-Gris Grits
Bamboula Tomato Cups
Baked Plantains

BROILED GRAPEFRUIT LAVEAU

3 grapefruit
6 heaping tsp. honey

Halve grapefruit. Remove core; seed and section with paring knife. Place 1 heaping teaspoon of honey on top of prepared grapefruit.

Preheat broiler. Place grapefruit halves under direct flame. Broil for about 5 minutes or until edges brown. Serve immediately. Serves six.

EGGS BENE-LOX

1 egg
1 slice toast or ½ toasted
   English muffin
sour cream

1 tbsp. Hollandaise Sauce
   (see recipe)
1 slice lox
kosher caviar

Soak toast in sour cream and place in ramekins or small baking dish. Cover toast with lox and break egg on top. Bake in 350-degree oven for about 12 to 15 minutes or until egg is set.

Remove from baking dish. Add Hollandaise Sauce and sprinkle with caviar. Serve immediately. Serves one.

HOLLANDAISE SAUCE

¼ cup pareve margarine
1 egg yolk
½ tbsp. lemon juice

⅛ tsp. salt
dash cayenne

Place yolk with ⅓ of margarine in top of double boiler. Keep water in bottom of boiler hot but not boiling. Stir egg and margarine constantly. When margarine melts, add another portion butter until mixture thickens. Add remaining margarine and keep stirring.

When thick, remove from heat and add salt and cayenne. Should sauce separate, beat in 1 tablespoon boiling water, drop by drop. Serve immediately over desired vegetable. Makes one half cup.

FRIED GRITS

Pour cooked grits into 8½- by 4½- by 2½-inch loaf pan and cool slightly. Cover and refrigerate several hours or overnight.

Cut chilled grits in 12 sections. Fry over medium heat in small amount of butter in cast-iron skillet until golden brown (about 10 minutes per side).

For a richer, browner color, dip slices of grits in beaten egg before frying. Serves six.

CREOLE-STYLE TOMATOES

6 medium-size creole
  tomatoes
½ cup fine, dry bread
  crumbs or flour

½ tsp. salt
dash pepper
shortening

Cut tomatoes crosswise into ½-inch-thick slices. Dip each slice in combined crumbs, salt, and pepper. Fry in small amount of shortening until brown on both sides (about 10 minutes). (For a delicious variation, dip tomatoes in cornmeal.) Serves six.

SABRA CREPES

1 cup sifted confectioners'
  sugar
2 tbsp. Sabra liqueur (or any
  brand of kosher orange
  liqueur)
1 egg yolk

1 cup milk
3 egg yolks, well beaten
½ cup sifted cake flour
1 tbsp. sugar
1 tsp. salt

FILLING:

Thoroughly blend sugar and 1 tbsp. liqueur. Add mixture to well-beaten egg yolk to make a paste, beating until smooth (about the thickness of mayonnaise).

CREPES:

Combine milk and egg yolks. Mix flour with sugar and salt. Add liquid mixture to dry ingredients, and mix thoroughly. Preheat griddle to medium heat and grease lightly with butter. Use about ¼ cup batter for each crepe. (Crepes should be thin and about 5 inches in diameter.) When edges of crepe begin to brown, turn and brown other side.

When crepe is done, place spoonful of filling near center. Fold over filling at sides and ends. Place on a heat-proof serving dish and bake in a 400-degree oven for 5 minutes or until lightly brown. Crepes will puff slightly.

Remove from oven and sprinkle with additional confectioners' sugar. Pour 1 tbsp. liqueur over crepes, light with match, and allow flame to burn down. Serve immediately. Serves eight.

CAFÉ BRÛLOT

1½ cups brandy
2 strips lemon peel
1 strip orange peel
8 whole cloves

8 whole allspice
2 2-inch sticks cinnamon
8 cubes sugar
3 cups strong, hot coffee

Mix brandy, lemon and orange peel, cloves, allspice, and cinnamon in pan; heat through and drain. Remove peels and spices from brandy mixture. Add 7 cubes sugar to brandy mixture and place remaining cube in a ladle. Place small amount of brandy mixture in ladle and ignite. Lower ladle into a chafing dish carefully and ignite entire brandy mixture.

Stir carefully with the ladle, dipping and pouring back into pan, until sugar is dissolved.

Pour hot coffee slowly against edge of chafing dish. Ladle into demitasse cups when mixture is no longer flaming. Serve with additional sugar, if desired. Makes sixteen demitasse.

GALLERY BISCUITS

2 cups sifted flour
3 tsp. baking powder
½ tsp. salt

⅓ cup vegetable shortening
½ cup nondairy creamer
¼ cup water

Preheat oven to 475°. Sift flour, baking powder, and salt together and cut in shortening. Add liquid and mix well.

Knead on floured board about 20 times. Roll out ¼ inch thick. Cut with biscuit cutter dipped in flour. Place 1 inch apart on lightly greased cookie sheet. Bake 8 to 10 minutes. Makes about two dozen biscuits.

VIEUX CARRÉ SPINACH SALAD

1 lb. fresh spinach
¼ cup sugar
1 tsp. finely grated onion
6 slices Beef Frye cooked
  until crisp, drained and
  crumbled
½ cup salad oil

2 tbsp. vinegar
½ tsp. salt
¼ tsp. dry mustard
5 hard-cooked eggs,
  chopped
1 hard-cooked egg, sliced

Wash spinach thoroughly in water; drain. Chill to crisp.

Combine oil, sugar, vinegar, onion, salt, and mustard. Beat or blend in blender until dressing becomes thick and syrupy and sugar is thoroughly dissolved.

Tear spinach in bite-size portions and place in large salad bowl. Add Beef Frye and chopped eggs. Pour dressing over salad and let stand about ½ hour. Toss and garnish with egg slices. Serves six.

VOO-DEN VEAL GRILLADES

2 lbs. ½-inch-thick veal
  shoulder
6 tbsp. schmaltz
2 cups chopped onion
½ cup chopped green
  pepper
2 cloves garlic, minced
1 cup chopped tomato

½ tsp. dried thyme
4 tbsp. flour
2¼ cups water
2 tbsp. chopped parsley
2 tsp. salt
¼ tsp. pepper
¼ tsp. Tabasco sauce

Cut meat into serving-size pieces and pound with mallet until ¼ inch thick. Heat 4 tbsp. schmaltz in large skillet over medium heat. Sauté meat until brown (about 5 minutes each side). Remove meat to a platter.

Lower heat and sauté onion, green pepper, garlic, tomato, and thyme until light brown (8 to 10 minutes), stirring frequently. Remove vegetables to meat platter. Increase heat and add remaining schmaltz. Stir in flour and cook until dark brown, stirring constantly.

Lower heat and gradually add 1¼ cups water, stirring to blend. Add parsley, 1 tsp. salt, meat, and vegetables. Cover and cook over low heat 30 minutes. Add additional salt and pepper to taste; stir in remaining water as needed. Cover and continue cooking slowly until meat is tender (about 45 minutes). Stir occasionally. (Delicious served with hot grits.) Serves four.

GRIS-GRIS GRITS

⅔ cup white hominy grits
¾ tsp. salt
3⅓ cups boiling water (or
   2⅓ cups water mixed
   with 1 cup nondairy
   cream, brought to a boil)

Stir grits slowly into boiling salted water in heavy saucepan. Return to boil; reduce heat and cover. Cook slowly for 25 to 30 minutes, stirring occasionally.

Serve with butter as side dish for breakfast or as an accompaniment to smothered liver. (If served with liver, prepare with nondairy cream and water, and use pareve margarine on grits.) Serves four.

KOSHER CREOLE COOKBOOK

BAMBOULA TOMATO CUPS

¾ cup bread crumbs
2 tbsp. pareve margarine
6 medium creole tomatoes
½ tsp. salt
pepper to taste

1 cup cooked whole-kernel
  corn
¾ cup canned or cooked
  fresh mushrooms

Sauté bread crumbs in margarine until brown. Cut thin slices from stem ends of tomatoes and remove pulp, reserving 1 cup.

Combine salt, pepper, corn, mushrooms, reserved tomato pulp, and ½ cup bread crumbs. Fill tomatoes with corn mixture and sprinkle with remaining crumbs. Place in a baking dish and bake at 350° for 30 minutes. Serves six.

BAKED PLANTAINS

6 plantains, peeled
finely chopped nuts,
  cinnamon, or coconut

¼ cup melted pareve
  margarine

Brush plantains with margarine. Sprinkle with cinnamon, nuts, or coconut. Bake 15 to 20 minutes at 375° until hot and tender; do not overbake. Serve hot. Serves six.

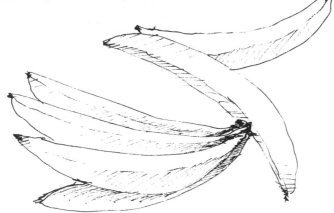

December

December

Patio Potpourri

New Orleans' picturesque patios, predominantly located in the Vieux Carré, are frequented in most tours of the city. The Creoles considered it a breach of etiquette to enter their homes through the front door. They entered on the side by means of a patio or courtyard, passing through a *porte cochère*, a wide gate high enough to allow a coachman wearing his high hat to remain seated on the carriage. Patio is the Spanish equivalent of courtyard, and in French derives from the phrase *coeur de maison*, meaning "heart of the house."

Folklore relates an interesting interpretation of the origin of the word "patio." As the horsedrawn carriages pulled into the opened gates, the hoof-beats gradually slowed to a "pat-a-pat-pat," and the cry of "whoa, whoa" was heard until the carriage came to a stop. In imitation of the two sounds, the combination "pat-pat" and "whoa" soon became slurred, and the word "patio" emerged.

Surrounded by the raised main living quarters and usually encased in a u-shaped railed gallery from where the main doors opened, this area was the heart of the home. Here one could step out to view those who came to call. The architectural arrangement was most convenient for rejecting or welcoming the approaching visitor. As the servant looked down to see and announce the guest, members of the family decided whether they would come forth (a sign of welcome), or if the doors would remain closed (a sign of rejection).

One of the main features of the patio was the open hearth kitchen. As a safety measure after two devastating Vieux Carré fires in 1788 and 1794, the Spanish building code encouraged the building of kitchens separate from the main house. Often adjoining the patio (where culinary plants were grown and picked fresh as needed), these kitchens also kept heat out of the main house during hot, humid weather.

Apart from its many uses, the patio itself is a charming structure. Within the quiet seclusion of old brick walls, grey flagstone walks laid by slave labor remain intact. Growing in profusion are lush palmetto palms, banana trees, and tropical foliage, with wisteria and gardenia blooms sweetening the warm, still air.

Nothing was, or is today, more relaxing and refreshing than a light repast amidst these beautiful Southern settings. Serve a Kosher Creole potpourri (originally a stew, but later taken to mean a miscellaneous mixture or collection) and conclude with café au lait (coffee with chicory and hot milk) and beignets (hot fritters or light, airy doughnuts) sprinkled with powdered sugar. We call it Southern hospitality—Kosher Creole style!

December

I.

Mint Julep
Chicken Liver Paté
Potpourri Salad
French Dressing
Patio Bananas
Café Noir

II.

Absinthe Frappé
Porte Cochère Casserole
Brown Roux
Courtyard Salad
Corn Bread
Beignets

MINT JULEP

1 cup mint leaves
8 tsp. sugar
8 oz. bourbon (about 1½
   jiggers per glass)

4 tsp. confectioners' sugar
2 cups shaved ice

Place four glasses in refrigerator to chill. Rinse mint leaves and crush; mix with sugar. Place ¼ cup mint in bottom of each glass. Pour in 1½ jiggers bourbon, add ½ cup shaved ice, and stir with swizzle stick. Sprinkle teaspoon of confectioners' sugar on top of each drink and garnish with additional whole mint leaves. Serve with straw. Makes four drinks.

CHICKEN LIVER PATÉ

1 lb. chicken livers
3 hard-cooked eggs
salt and pepper
2 medium onions

2 tbsp. melted schmaltz
dash Worcestershire sauce
melba toast, party rye, or
   crackers

Salt and pepper livers. Broil under highest flame, just long enough to singe edges. Remove and set aside.

Chop 1 onion fine and sauté in small amount of schmaltz. Remove with slotted spoon. Add livers and sauté about 10 minutes or until done. Remove and set aside to cool.

In large wooden bowl, chop cooked and raw onion, eggs, and livers fine. Add dash of Worcestershire and enough melted schmaltz to make mixture moist enough to spread. Mix thoroughly. Adjust salt and pepper to taste. Spread on melba toast, party rye, or crackers. Makes about one cup.

POTPOURRI SALAD

½ lb. wild rice
4 cups chopped cooked
  chicken
1 cup mayonnaise
½ cup French Dressing (see
  recipe)
salt and pepper to taste

1 5-oz. can sliced almonds
1 cup diced celery
2 11-oz. cans mandarin
  oranges, drained
1 20-oz. can pineapple
  chunks, drained

Cook rice according to directions on package. Drain and cool. Add chopped chicken, mayonnaise, French dressing, salt, pepper, almonds, and celery. Mix well and chill.

Add oranges and pineapple just before serving and toss lightly. Serve on lettuce leaves. Serves four.

FRENCH DRESSING

½ cup olive oil
1 tsp. salt
2 cloves garlic, minced
paprika

1 cup tarragon vinegar
½ tsp. pepper
¼ tsp. onion powder

Mix ingredients in pint jar. Add enough paprika to make mixture a dark orange color. Shake well and refrigerate. (Best when made a day or so before using, to allow garlic to marinate. Will stay fresh indefinitely in refrigerator.) Makes one pint.

PATIO BANANAS

1 tbsp. cornstarch
2 tbsp. sugar
2⅓ cups nondairy creamer
4 egg yolks, slightly beaten

1 tsp. vanilla
6 bananas, peeled
nutmeg (optional)

Mix cornstarch and sugar in top of double boiler. Stir in nondairy creamer. Place top of double boiler over low direct heat. Stir constantly until mixture thickens slightly. Remove from heat and stir a small amount of hot nondairy mixture into beaten yolks.

Place top of double boiler back over hot water; cook mixture, stirring constantly, until thick and smooth. Remove from heat and stir in vanilla. Cool; then chill.

Cut peeled bananas into chunks and place in dessert dishes or large bowl. Pour custard sauce over banana pieces, sprinkle with nutmeg, and serve at once. Serves six.

CAFÉ NOIR

Place 2 tablespoons coffee with chicory in drip coffeepot for each cup of water used. Add 2 tablespoons boiling water over grounds every few minutes until desired amount of coffee is brewed.

ABSINTHE FRAPPÉ

1 tsp. simple syrup (see recipe)
2 oz. absinthe (Pernod or Herbsaint)

dash club soda

Shake well and pour over cracked ice. Top with club soda. Makes one 3-ounce frappé.

Simple Syrup

1 cup water
2 cups sugar
3 or 4 slices of lemon

Combine ingredients and heat in a saucepan for five minutes.

PORTE COCHÈRE CASSEROLE

2 lbs. smoked trout
2 tbsp. butter or pareve
  margarine
2 shallots, minced
2 tbsp. flour
2½-oz. can mushroom
  stems and pieces,
  drained, or ¼ cup cooked
  fresh mushrooms,
  chopped

dash cayenne pepper
½ tsp. salt
1 tbsp. Worcestershire
  sauce
½ tsp. chopped parsley
1 egg yolk
bread crumbs
⅛ tsp. nutmeg (optional)

Sauté onions in Brown Roux (see recipe). Remove skin and bones from trout and flake in large pieces. Add trout pieces, mushroom pieces, salt, pepper, Worcestershire sauce, and parsley to roux. Cook 10 minutes over medium heat, stirring occasionally.

Remove from heat and add egg yolk and nutmeg. Mix well. Spoon mixture into six ramekins and cover with bread crumbs. Dot with additional butter or margarine. Bake at 350° for 15 minutes. Serves six.

BROWN ROUX

2 tbsp. shortening
2 tbsp. flour

Heat shortening. Add flour, stirring slowly until brown; salt and pepper to taste.

Roux is the basis for most Creole cooking and is used in many different kinds of recipes.

COURTYARD SALAD

1 8-oz. jar herring tidbits
   in wine sauce, drained
2 heads romaine lettuce
2 creole tomatoes
1 green pepper
3 shallots, cut up
3 hard-cooked eggs
1 small dill pickle

3 stuffed pimento olives
2 tbsp. minced celery hearts
1 tsp. Tabasco sauce
salt and pepper to taste
2 tbsp. French Dressing (see
   recipe)
watercress for garnish

Chop herring tidbits very fine. Mash egg yolks. Combine herring, yolks, French dressing, and Tabasco sauce to make smooth paste.

Mince olives, pickles, egg whites, and celery together. Set aside.

Place leaves of lettuce and watercress on large platter. Slice tomatoes and green pepper and place with shallots in center of platter. Spread herring paste over this and sprinkle with minced olives, pickle, egg whites, and celery. Salt and pepper to taste. Chill before serving. Serves four.

CORN BREAD

1 cup yellow cornmeal
¼ cup sugar
½ tsp. salt
1 cup milk (or ½ cup water and ½ cup nondairy creamer)

1 cup sifted all-purpose flour
4 tsp. baking powder
1 egg
¼ cup softened shortening

Sift together cornmeal, flour, sugar, baking powder, and salt into bowl. Add egg, milk (or substitute), and shortening. Beat wth rotary beater until smooth (about 1 minute). Bake in greased 8-inch-square baking pan in preheated 425-degree oven for 20 to 25 minutes. (To make corn sticks or muffins, pour corn-bread batter into hot greased corn-stick pans or muffin cups. Bake in preheated 425-degree oven for 15 to 20 minutes.) Serves 8 or 9.

BEIGNETS

½ cup boiling water
2 tbsp. vegetable shortening
¼ cup sugar
½ tsp. salt
½ cup evaporated milk
½ pkg. yeast

¼ cup warm water
1 egg, beaten
3¾ cups sifted flour
1 cup sifted confectioners' sugar

Pour boiling water over shortening, sugar, and salt. Add milk and let stand until warm. Dissolve yeast in ¼ cup warm water; add yeast and egg to milk mixture.

Stir in about 2 cups flour and beat well. Add enough additional flour to make a soft dough. Place in greased bowl; grease top of dough and cover with waxed paper and a dry cloth. Place in refrigerator until ready to use.

Roll dough to ¼-inch thickness. Work quickly so dough does not rise before frying. Cut into 2½-inch squares. Heat deep fat to 360° in heavy skillet or deep fryer. Drop squares into fat a few at a time allowing room for expansion. Brown on one side and then the other, turning only once. Drain on absorbent paper. Sprinkle with confectioners' sugar while still warm, or shake beignets in brown bag with sugar. Serve immediately. Makes about thirty beignets.

January

January

Sugar Bowl Soirées

Along with its fine cuisine, Louisiana boasts of being a sportsman's paradise. Foremost in Louisiana's claim to fame in the sports world is the annual Sugar Bowl classic held in New Orleans on New Year's Day. It ranks as a major event in the realm of contemporary American amateur football.

As a result of the vision and determination of its thirty-nine original organizers, the New Orleans Mid-Winter Sports Association was founded in October 1934. Their baby was christened in Tulane Stadium in 1936 when the universities of Tulane and Temple competed before 22,026 delighted spectators to the tune of over $40,000 in gate receipts.

The Sugar Bowl grew and grew. The increased demand for tickets eventually brought about the enlargement of Tulane Stadium; 14,000 additional seats were constructed to accommodate the expanding number of fans. Continued requests soon resulted in a stadium with a capacity of over 70,000 seats.

As the brainchild of the New Orleans Mid-Winter Association grew, so did the number of events associated with the Sugar Bowl. A week-long series of sports attractions including basketball games, boxing matches, regattas, tennis matches, and track meets soon became an established part of Sugar Bowl week.

Today Louisiana's phenomenal Superdome is the site of the Sugar Bowl classic. An indoor temperature-controlled arena seating almost 100,000, it features many advantages of modern technology: instant replay screens, artificial turf, electric score boards, loud speakers. The half-time shows rival Broadway productions and Las Vegas revues, and, of course, concession stands are located throughout the multilevel structure (after all, in New Orleans, food is a *must* for *all* activities).

As visitors from every state in the union flock to the city for Sugar Bowl week, local residents vie as fiercely for championship status on the dining table as do the starring teams on the field. Hosts throughout the city are engaged in a series of *soirées* (which is what Creoles called an evening at home with guests); brunches before the game, buffets and dinners after the game, and midnight "victory" snacks. Everywhere the charm, tradition, and even some of the old dietary superstitions can be seen and tasted—cabbage dishes (believed to bring money and riches in the new year) and black-eyed peas (thought to bring good luck).

In the manner of true Southern hospitality, we invite you to a *soirée*. With these recipes, your guests may demand some "instant replates" and you may run extra yards back and forth to your kitchen to fulfill their requests; but one thing is certain—you'll score heavily on compliments sweeter than the contents of any Sugar Bowl.

January
Pre-Game Buffet

Classic Cole Slaw
Sugar Bowl Avocado Spread
Gefilte Fish Fritters
Baked Cheese Grits
Le Bon Black-Eyed Peas
Quiche Lorraine
Dixie Drop Biscuits
Fig Preserves
Superdome Café Ring

After-Game Dinner

Kick Off Salad
Oysters Moskawitz
Veal Jambalaya
Touchdown Smothered Cabbage
Stadium Okra and Tomatoes
Ma Mère Pecan Pie

Midnight Victory Snack

Egg Nog
Sportsman's Salad
Kosher Creole Seafood Gumbo
Winner's Almond Torte

CLASSIC COLE SLAW

2½ cups shredded green
  cabbage
1 cup shredded red cabbage
1 carrot, shredded
¾ cup celery, diced fine

1 tbsp. lemon juice
salt and pepper to taste
3 tbsp. salad oil
½ cup mayonnaise

Combine all ingredients and refrigerate in covered bowl until ready to serve. Serves six to eight.

SUGAR BOWL AVOCADO SPREAD

1 16-oz. jar pickled
  herring tidbits, drained
  and finely chopped
1 tsp. wine vinegar
¼ cup mayonnaise
2 medium ripe avocados,
  peeled and chopped

½ apple, peeled and finely
  chopped
1 tsp. mustard
1 small onion, finely
  chopped

Mix ingredients together and serve on crackers or party-rye slices. Makes about four cups.

GEFILTE FISH FRITTERS

1 6-oz. pkg. potato-
  pancake mix
1 8-oz. jar small gefilte-fish
  balls
3 cups vegetable oil

2 eggs
2¼ cups water
1 cup fresh or canned whole-
  kernel corn, drained

Combine potato-pancake mix with eggs and water as directed on package. Stir in corn and fish balls. Heat oil in a large skillet until it reaches 375°. Drop heaping tablespoon of batter into hot oil and fry until golden brown on both sides, turning only once. Drain on paper towels. Serve with applesauce or sour cream. Makes eighteen fritters.

BAKED CHEESE GRITS

5 cups water, lightly
  salted
½ cup softened butter
1 tbsp. Worcestershire
  sauce
1 cup grits

2½ cups grated sharp
  cheddar cheese
3 eggs, slightly beaten
salt and cayenne pepper to
  taste

Bring water to boil in large, heavy saucepan. Sprinkle in grits, stir, and let water return to boil. Reduce heat to low, cover, and cook grits, stirring occasionally for 25 to 30 minutes or until liquid is absorbed and mixture is thick. Remove pan from heat and let cool for 10 minutes.

Stir in cheese and butter, eggs, Worcestershire sauce, salt, and cayenne. Pour mixture into buttered 2-quart casserole and bake in preheated 350-degree oven for 1 hour or until it becomes puffy and brown. Serves eight.

LE BON BLACK-EYED PEAS

4 tbsp. pareve margarine
½ cup fresh or canned
  tomatoes, chopped

1 16-oz. can black-eyed
  peas
1 16-oz. can cut snap beans

Drain liquid from peas and beans, reserving ¼ cup from each can. Combine melted margarine, tomatoes, peas, beans, and ½ cup liquid. Pour into 1½-quart baking dish. Cover and bake in 350-degree oven for 25 minutes. Serves four to five.

QUICHE LORRAINE

1 9-inch unbaked pie shell
imitation bacon bits
12 slices Swiss cheese
4 eggs
1 tbsp. flour

⅛ tsp. cayenne pepper
½ tsp. salt
1 pt. half-and-half
1½ tbsp. butter
⅛ tsp. nutmeg (optional)

Bake pie shell until light brown (do not overbake) and allow to cool; line with cheese.

Combine eggs, flour, salt, cayenne, nutmeg, cream, and melted butter. Pour over cheese and bake at 375° for 45 minutes or until mixture is set and evenly browned. (To test, insert knife in center of custard. If knife comes out clean, it has set.) Sprinkle imitation bacon bits over top and serve. Serves six.

DIXIE DROP BISCUITS

1 cup all-purpose flour
1½ tsp. baking powder
2 tbsp. shortening

½ tsp. salt
½ cup milk

Sift together dry ingredients; cut in shortening, and stir in milk. Drop by the tablespoon onto greased cookie sheet (about 2 inches apart). Bake eight to ten minutes in 475-degree oven. Makes eighteen to twenty biscuits.

FIG PRESERVES

2 qts. fresh figs　　　　　　　4 cups sugar
2 cups water　　　　　　　　1 sliced lemon
2 cinnamon sticks

Wash figs and remove stems. Combine sugar and water in large saucepan. Heat, stirring until sugar is dissolved. Add lemon slices, cinnamon sticks, and figs; cook slowly until figs are tender and transparent (about 1½ to 2 hours). Remove figs with slotted spoon. Continue to cook syrup until it reaches the soft-ball stage (230 degrees on candy thermometer).

Fill sterilized pint jars about ¾ full with figs; pour in enough syrup to cover figs completely, leaving about ½ inch at top of jar. Seal. Makes two pints.

SUPERDOME CAFÉ RING

2 cakes yeast　　　　　　　　1 cup scalded milk
¼ cup lukewarm water　　　　1 tsp. grated lemon rind
¼ cup shortening　　　　　　5 cups sifted flour
½ cup sugar　　　　　　　　½ cup ground pecans
1 tsp. salt　　　　　　　　　1 cup brown sugar
½ cup raisins　　　　　　　　maraschino cherries and
½ tsp. cinnamon　　　　　　　　halved pecans for
2 eggs, beaten　　　　　　　　　decoration

Soften yeast in lukewarm water. Add shortening, sugar, and salt to scalded milk; cool until lukewarm. Add softened yeast, eggs, lemon rind, and enough flour to make a stiff batter. Beat well; add more flour (enough to make a soft dough).

Turn out on lightly floured board and knead until smooth and dough takes on a satiny sheen. Place in greased bowl, cover, and let rise until doubled in bulk (about 1 hour). Punch down and shape into 2 rectangular sheets about ¼ inch thick. Brush with melted butter and sprinkle with brown sugar, cinnamon, ground pecans, and raisins. Roll from long end as you would a jelly roll. Shape into ring and pinch ends together. Place on greased baking sheet and cut with scissors at 1-inch intervals almost through ring. Fan out slices slightly. Cover and let rise until doubled in bulk (about 1 hour).

Bake in 375-degree oven for 25 to 30 minutes. While warm, spread top with Icing (see recipe) and sprinkle with chopped pecans. Decorate with pecan halves and cherries. Makes two rings.

ICING:

2 cups confectioners' sugar
1 tsp. vanilla extract
4 tbsp. warm milk

Mix thoroughly and spread on ring.

KICK OFF SALAD

1 lb. fresh green beans
2 tsp. salt
½ cup salad oil
½ cup lemon juice
1 tsp. dry mustard
freshly ground pepper to
taste

dash of cayenne pepper
1 hard-cooked egg yolk,
riced
2 tbsp. capers

Wash beans; remove ends and strings. Bring 1 inch of water to boil in a large saucepan. Add whole beans and 1 teaspoon salt and cook for 5 minutes. Cover, reduce heat, and simmer for 10 minutes; drain.

Combine oil, lemon juice, remaining salt, mustard, pepper, and cayenne pepper. Place beans in large bowl and pour dressing over them. Toss lightly and cool.

Cover and place in refrigerator for at least 2 hours. Drain and place beans on salad plates. Garnish with egg yolk and capers. Serves four to six.

OYSTERS MOSKAWITZ

2 1-lb. cans salmon
6 shallots, chopped
1½ tbsp. Worcestershire
  sauce
1 clove garlic, chopped

2 cups seasoned bread
  crumbs
additional salt and pepper
  to taste
¼ lb. pareve margarine

*Drain juices from salmon and set aside. Place salmon in deep bowl.
Mix shallots, garlic, Worcestershire sauce, salt, pepper, and margarine
and cook in skillet until well blended (about 5 to 10 minutes). Put
salmon back in skillet and simmer until done (about 10 minutes). Add
bread crumbs and enough salmon liquid until moist but not loose. Place
in ramekins while hot and serve. Serves six.*

VEAL JAMBALAYA

1½ cups cooked rice
2 tbsp. pareve margarine
3 cups cooked veal, cut in
  1-inch cubes
3 shallots, chopped
1 slice pimento
2 hard-cooked eggs,
  chopped

1 bouillon cube
1 cup boiling water
2 egg yolks
1 cup nondairy creamer
1 tsp. salt
¼ tsp. white pepper

*Dissolve bouillon cube in water. Heat margarine in skillet and sauté
shallots until soft; add veal and rice. Stir until thoroughly heated; then
add pimento, hard-cooked eggs, and bouillon. Cook for 5 minutes on
low heat, stirring gently to blend.*

*Mix nondairy creamer with egg yolks, salt, and pepper until well
blended. Add to veal and stir until mixture thickens. Serves six.*

TOUCHDOWN SMOTHERED CABBAGE

1 small onion, chopped
¼ lb. salami or hot sausage
1 head cabbage, coarsely
  chopped

1 tsp. salt
½ tsp. pepper
1 tbsp. pareve margarine

Sauté onion and meat in margarine. Add cabbage (with water still clinging to leaves from washing), salt, and pepper. Cover and cook over low heat for about 1½ to 2 hours. Serves four to six.

STADIUM OKRA AND TOMATOES

2 qts. sliced fresh okra
4 fresh tomatoes, peeled
  and diced
1 medium green pepper,
  chopped

1 medium onion, chopped
5 tbsp. olive oil
salt and pepper to taste

Heat olive oil in large heavy skillet or pot and sauté onion and green pepper until light brown. Add okra and tomatoes and season to taste with salt and pepper. Cover and cook over low heat 30 to 40 minutes, stirring occasionally. Serves six.

MA MÈRE PECAN PIE

1 9-inch pie crust,
  unbaked
1 cup Karo syrup (blue label)
1 cup sugar
1 cup pecans
2 eggs, beaten

⅛ tsp. salt
1 tsp. vanilla
2 tbsp. melted pareve
  margarine

Mix ingredients together, adding pecans last. Pour into pastry shell. Bake in 400-degree oven for 40 minutes or until a silver knife inserted in center of filling comes out clean. Cool on wire rack.

EGG NOG

1 qt. milk
4 eggs, separated
½ cup sugar

nutmeg and whiskey to
taste

Scald milk. Beat egg yolks and sugar until creamy. Add small amount of scalded milk to egg mixture and stir. Combine egg mixture with remaining milk and stir and cook on low heat until thoroughly blended. Beat egg whites until stiff and fold in. Add nutmeg and whiskey. Serves four.

SPORTSMAN'S SALAD

3 cups grated carrots
1 8¼-oz. can crushed
   pineapple, drained

½ cup seedless raisins
¼ cup chopped celery
½ cup mayonnaise

Combine ingredients and chill. Serve on lettuce leaves. Serves six.

KOSHER CREOLE SEAFOOD GUMBO

1 large onion, chopped
½ green pepper, chopped
1 clove garlic, minced
2 tbsp. vegetable oil
2 tbsp. flour
1 15-oz. can stewed
   tomatoes
1 6-oz. can tomato paste
2 tsp. salt
1 bay leaf
½ tsp. chili powder

½ tsp. basil leaves
1 lb. trout fillets
1 10-oz. pkg. frozen sliced
   okra, partially thawed, or
   1 lb. fresh okra, sliced
½ lb. redfish fillets
3 cups water
1 tbsp. Worcestershire
   sauce
3 cups hot cooked rice

Sauté vegetables slightly in oil in Dutch oven. Stir in flour; blend well. Add remaining ingredients except fish, okra, and rice. Simmer covered for 30 minutes.

Remove bay leaf. Add fish and okra. Cover and simmer additional 10 to 15 minutes or until okra is tender. Serve in soup bowls over hot cooked rice. Serves six to eight.

WINNER'S ALMOND TORTE

8 tbsp. butter or pareve margarine
1 cup light brown sugar
½ tsp. almond extract
1 egg

5 tbsp. enriched flour
½ cup chopped pecans
½ cup chopped almonds
1 cup whipped heavy cream

Cream butter and sugar; add almond extract, egg, and flour. Blend well and add nuts. Shape into roll, wrap in aluminum foil, and place in freezer.

When ready to serve, thaw about 30 minutes. Slice 1 inch thick and top with whipped cream. Decorate with slivered almonds or additional chopped pecans. Serves six to eight.

February

February

Mardi Gras Masquerades

It is little wonder that New Orleans is also known as "the city that Care forgot." If you have ever witnessed Mardi Gras you can readily understand this sobriquet.

There is a distinction between Mardi Gras and Carnival. The Carnival Season begins on January 6 (Twelfth Night) and continues through Mardi Gras. Festivities begin even before Christmas, and Carnival encompasses the entire season of parades, balls, and social affairs associated with Mardi Gras. Mardi Gras is one day only—Fat Tuesday or Shrove Tuesday, the day before Lent. The two terms are, however, used interchangeably; Mardi Gras is referred to as Carnival Day and Carnival as Mardi Gras.

The first Carnival organization came into being in 1857, calling itself the Mystick Krewe of Comus. A group of men gathered together simply to have one more fling before the beginning of the solemn Lenten season. They soon found themselves outdoors, joyfully parading in the streets to the delight of onlookers.

With the influx of newcomers as the city grew, the Americans added to the excitement of the Carnival season. Using their organizational, economic, and creative expertise, they turned Mardi Gras into a festive, frenzied, city-wide celebration. It is wild. It is hectic. In other words, Mardi Gras is a contagious fever that sweeps over the city in epidemic proportions infecting those from all stations of life.

Today parades begin two weeks before Mardi Gras Day, often with as many as five parades on a single day. The night parades with their *flambeaux* (flaming torches) carriers, floats bearing masked riders tossing favors or throws to the uplifted arms of thousands, the marching bands interspersed with horseback riders atop intricately designed saddles, masqueraders dancing in the streets, and the shouts of "Throw me somethin' mista" all belong to the masses.

The banners and streamers strung across balconies, galleries, and porches bear the Mardi Gras colors: purple, for justice; green, for faith; and gold, for power. The anthem of Mardi Gras, "If Ever I Cease to Love," accompanies the Lord of Misrule and is played by his royal musicians continuously throughout the day.

From the time Rex, the king of Mardi Gras, takes to the streets on the morning of Fat Tuesday to lead the endless procession of floats and decorated trucks, it is a nonstop, anything-goes affair until the mad-cap climax at the stroke of midnight—the time when, as in the story of Cinderella, the pumpkin that is Mardi Gras and the wall-to-wall carpet of humanity that is Canal Street, revert from a world of make-believe to the realism of everyday living.

Mardi Gras and the entire Carnival season is one gigantic party. Everyone adds their own spice not only to their food but also to having fun. Mardi Gras is a favorite date on the New Orleans calendar, and probably the most important when it comes to entertaining.

Take a tip from two Mardi Gras "mavens" (those in the know). If you're not one of those lucky ones who knows someone on the route, then pack the food baskets and cram the brown bags with enough to last the day long. Begin your preparations early and join in the fun of the big day.

February

I.

Parade Punch
Pickled Mirlitons
Pickled Okra
Eggplant Fantasy
Mardi Gras Salad
Chicken and Sausage Jambalaya
Krewe Kugel
Kosher King's Cake
Queen's Pecan Bars

II.

Carnival Cucumbers
Boeuf Gras Burgers
Maskers' Fried Chicken
Rex's Red Bean Relish
Marching Band Brownies
Flambeaux Pecan Glazé

PARADE PUNCH

1 fifth of bourbon
1½ qts. orange juice
1 qt. lime juice
1 cup lemon juice
1 16-oz. bottle red cherries

2 16-oz. cans pineapple
chunks, or 1 fresh
pineapple, pared, cored,
and cut in chunks

Mix ingredients together and freeze. Thaw for 1 hour before serving. Garnish punch bowl with orange slices. (Prepare a day or so before serving and place in the freezer. Any leftovers can be refrozen.) Makes about five quarts.

PICKLED MIRLITONS

5 to 6 medium-size
  mirlitons
1 gal. red wine vinegar
1 qt. water

6 cloves garlic
1 cup salt
1 cup sugar
1 cup white mustard seed

Wash and peel mirlitons. Cut in strips or in eighths. Pack in sterilized jars with 1 clove garlic in each. Mix vinegar, water, salt, sugar, and mustard seed and bring to a boil. Pour hot vinegar solution over mirlitons. Seal at once. Makes six pints.

PICKLED OKRA

2 cups cider vinegar
1 tbsp. salt
2 tbsp. dill seed
½ tsp. Tabasco sauce
1 lb. fresh okra

2 cups water
2 tbsp. mustard seed
2 tbsp. celery seed
2 cloves garlic

Combine vinegar, water, salt, mustard seed, dill seed, celery seed, and Tabasco sauce in large kettle. Simmer 10 minutes.

Remove stem ends and place okra in 2 sterilized 12-oz. jars. Add 1 garlic clove to each jar and fill with pickling liquid. Seal and store at least 3 weeks. Makes two twelve-oz. jars.

EGGPLANT FANTASY

6 small eggplants
5 medium-size white
   onions, finely minced
2 cloves garlic, finely
   minced

1 cup olive oil
½ cup tarragon vinegar
½ tsp. Tabasco sauce
1 tsp. salt.

Bake eggplants in 350-degree oven until skins are very dark and wrinkled. Remove and cool.

Drain and peel eggplants and mash very fine. Add minced onions and garlic and mix well. Add salt and Tabasco sauce, then olive oil a little at a time, blending well. Add vinegar gradually and blend well. Refrigerate for at least 2 hours. Serve with crackers or toast rounds. Makes about 2 cups.

MARDI GRAS SALAD

1 head fresh cauliflower
2 raw carrots
1 15-oz. can cut green beans
2 cups diced celery
1 2-oz. jar chopped pimento
2 small onions, diced fine
1 cup sugar

¾ cup vegetable oil
1½ tbsp. salt
pepper to taste
1 cup tarragon vinegar
1 green pepper, diced
   (optional)

Wash cauliflower and scrape carrots. Parboil each for 1 minute. Remove, drain, and cool. Break cauliflower into bite-size pieces. Slice carrots in ½-inch pieces. Drain juices from beans and pimento.

Mix all ingredients well and place in covered bowl in refrigerator. Allow at least 12 hours to marinate. Serves six.

CHICKEN AND SAUSAGE JAMBALAYA

1 2½-lb. chicken, cut up
4 tbsp. Beef-Frye drippings
4 stalks celery, minced
1 8-oz. can tomato sauce
1 10½-oz. can condensed
 kosher chicken soup,
 undiluted
1¾ cups water
1½ lbs. cubed kosher hot
 sausages
1 large onion, chopped

1 bell pepper, chopped
2 cloves garlic, minced
2 cups raw long-grain white
 rice
1 cup cut-up kosher smoked
 sausage
4 shallots, chopped
¼ cup chopped parsley
½ tsp. cayenne pepper
salt and pepper to taste

Brown chicken pieces in drippings. Remove chicken and sauté onion, bell pepper, celery, and garlic in drippings. Add tomato sauce, soup, water, and smoked sausages. Cover and let simmer for about 30 minutes.

Bring mixture to boil and add rice, chicken, hot sausages, shallots, parsley, cayenne, salt, and pepper. Cover and cook over low heat for 30 to 45 minutes, or until chicken is tender and rice is done. Serves six.

KREWE KUGEL

2 10½-oz. boxes pareve
 kosher cocktail crackers
2 medium onions
¾ cup melted pareve
 margarine
2 tbsp. minced parsley

4 medium carrots, pared
2 stalks celery
4 eggs, slightly beaten
1 can condensed clear
 chicken soup, undiluted
¼ tsp. pepper

Put crackers, carrots, onions, and celery through medium blade of meat grinder. Mix thoroughly with margarine, eggs, soup, parsley, and pepper. Spread in well-greased 8- by 12- by 2-inch baking pan. Bake in a 375-degree oven for 45 minutes or until well browned. Serves 8 to 10.

KOSHER KING'S CAKE

1 pkg. yeast
1/4 cup warm water
6 tbsp. scalded nondairy
   creamer
4 cups flour
1 cup pareve margarine

3/4 cup sugar
1/4 tsp. salt
4 eggs
1 tbsp. melted pareve
   margarine

Dissolve yeast in warm water. Add nondairy creamer and enough flour (about 1/2 cup) to make a soft dough.

In a separate bowl combine margarine, sugar, salt, and eggs with electric mixer on low speed. Add soft ball of yeast dough and mix thoroughly. Gradually add 2 1/2 cups flour to make a medium dough. Place in greased bowl and brush top of dough with melted margarine. Cover with damp cloth and let rise until doubled in bulk (about 3 hours).

Sprinkle 1 cup flour on board. Place dough on board and knead until smooth. Roll into long strand and twist. Place on greased cookie sheet and form into oval shape, connecting ends by pinching together with dampened fingers.

Cover with damp cloth and let rise until doubled in bulk (about 1 hour). Bake in 325-degree oven for 35 to 45 minutes or until lightly browned.

Decorate top of cake with light coating of cane syrup and sprinkle with alternate bands of purple-, green-, and gold-colored sugar. (To color sugar, add few drops of food coloring and shake in tightly covered jar.) Makes one cake.

QUEEN'S PECAN BARS

2 tbsp. butter
1 cup brown sugar
⅛ tsp. baking soda
1 tsp. vanilla

2 eggs, slightly beaten
5 tbsp. flour
1 cup chopped pecans
½ cup confectioners' sugar

Put butter in 9-inch square pan. Place in 350-degree oven for 3 minutes or until butter melts. Combine eggs, sugar, flour, soda, pecans, and vanilla with mixer. Pour egg and sugar mixture over melted butter. Do not stir.

Bake at 350° for 25 minutes. Allow to remain in pan 5 minutes. Turn out and cool on rack.

Cut into 3- by 1-inch sections and sift confectioners' sugar on top. Makes about twenty-four bars.

CARNIVAL CUCUMBERS

8 lbs. medium-size
  cucumbers
2 tbsp. salt
6 medium-size onions
1 qt. vinegar
1 tsp. dry mustard

2 tsp. mustard seeds
2 tsp. celery seeds
½ tsp. turmeric
2 cups sugar
crushed ice

Wash and cut unpeeled cucumbers in paper-thin slices, enough to measure 4 quarts. Place in large, flat pan and cover with salt and crushed ice. Let soak for about 3 hours; then drain well.

While cucumber slices soak, peel and slice onions very thin; place in large kettle, along with drained cucumbers and remaining ingredients. Bring to a boil; then remove from heat immediately.

Spoon vegetable slices into 8 sterilized pint jars or 4 quart jars, and fill completely with vinegar mixture. Seal securely. Let stand 3 weeks before using. Makes eight pints.

BOEUF GRAS BURGERS

1½ lbs. ground beef
2 tbsp. Worcestershire
   sauce
¼ tsp. oregano
½ tsp. Accent
1 pkg. onion soup mix

¼ tsp. garlic powder
1 egg
¼ tsp. parsley, minced
1 slice bread, soaked in
   water and squeezed out

    Beat egg. Add onion soup mix, garlic powder, parsley, oregano, and Worcestershire to egg and blend well. Add bread and mash until dissolved in mixture.
    Sprinkle meat with Accent. Pour egg mixture over meat; blend well and shape into patties. Place in broiler and brown on both sides. Makes about ten burgers.

MASKERS' FRIED CHICKEN

2 frying chickens, cut up
1 tsp. seasoned salt
1 tsp. lemon pepper
1 tsp. fried chicken
   seasoning

1 tbsp. paprika
2 cups flour
brown paper bag
vegetable oil for frying

    Wipe pieces of chicken after rinsing. Generously season with salt, pepper, fried chicken seasoning, and paprika. Place a few pieces of chicken and some flour in bag and shake until chicken is well coated. Repeat process for remaining pieces of chicken.
    Use deep fryer or iron skillet to cook chicken. Allow oil to get very hot but not boiling. (Test with cube of bread; if it browns immediately, oil is hot enough.) Place chicken in deep fryer or skillet a few pieces at a time. (Part of the chicken should protrude from oil.) Cover at once.
    Fry 10 minutes on each side. When brown on both sides, remove and drain on paper towel. Serves eight.

REX'S RED BEAN RELISH

3 shallots
1 tbsp. minced parsley
2 tbsp. wine vinegar
5 tbsp. salad oil

salt and pepper to taste
2 cups cold cooked red
  beans

Chop shallots fine, including tops. Add parsley, vinegar, and oil and season to taste. Pour over beans and pack in jars. Serves four.

MARCHING BAND BROWNIES

⅔ cup unsifted flour
½ tsp. baking powder
1 cup sugar
2 packets Baker's Redi-
  Blend chocolate
½ cup broken walnuts or
  pecans

¼ tsp. salt
2 eggs
⅓ cup soft pareve margarine
1 tsp. vanilla extract

Combine flour, salt, and baking powder; set aside. Beat eggs well; gradually blend in sugar. Beat in margarine, and Redi-Blend, then blend in the flour mixture. Stir in nuts and vanilla.

Pour into greased 8-inch square pan and bake at 350° about 25 minutes. Cool in pan; then cut in squares. Makes about twenty brownies.

FLAMBEAUX PECAN GLAZÉ

2 cups pecan halves
¼ tsp. salt
1 tsp. vanilla extract

2 cups sugar
¼ tsp. baking soda

Place nut halves close together in a shallow, buttered pan. Heat sugar in heavy iron skillet, stirring constantly until syrup reaches 300 degrees (hard-crack stage) on candy thermometer.

Remove from heat and quickly stir in salt, soda, and vanilla. Pour over nuts. Break into pieces when cold. Makes about one and a half pounds.

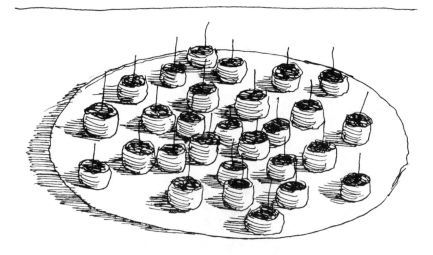

March

March

Jazz Jambalayas

There are many theories concerning the origin of jazz. But one fact we in New Orleans hold fast to: the music was born *here*, and will forever be identified with the city.

"Hot jazz"—with its faster tempo, harmony based on simple chords, an occasional added seventh or "blues" chord, and complicated further by improvisation—was first played by Negro bands in New Orleans around 1895. It was originally called ragtime, then "jass."

One theory has it that the word "jazz" was first known in the Creole argot as meaning "to speed up." Another interpretation claims darkest Africa as its origin with several references to words spelled variously *jas, jass,* and *jasz.* Yet another story deals with a man named Charles Washington. Charles, a drummer who lived in Vicksburg, Mississippi, around the turn of the century, was fondly nicknamed "Chaz." Whenever the leader of the small group with whom Chaz played felt the tempo was lagging, he would turn to his star percussionist and say, "*Now,* Chaz. *Now,* Chaz." From this story, it is easy to see how the word "jazz" may have come about.

Slaves found comfort in music. To make rhythms and sounds they whittled whistles from wood, used cigar boxes, and even filled gourds with pebbles. As the freed men began to earn money during the Reconstruction era, they were able to purchase instruments, primarily cornets, clarinets, and trumpets. They were self-taught musicians and created their own sounds and songs, a combination of lonesome wails, jungle beats, and rasping notes of the horn. Every sound they heard, from the whistle of the riverboat to the arias of the opera, was incorporated into their rhythmic interpretations.

Improvisation was their talent; each man was a soloist and together they were a team. Their unique sounds would later be recognized as America's contribution to music. The music of King Oliver, Jelly Roll Morton, Louis "Satchmo" Armstrong, Bix Beiderbecke, the Original Dixieland Band, Pete Fountain, and Al Hirt brings about an immediate impulse to snap your fingers, clap your hands, and tap your feet to the irresistible rhythm.

In 1970 the Jazz and Heritage Festival was instituted in New Orleans, affording talented people throughout the nation an opportunity to gather together in the city where jazz was born. The festival is dedicated to the tradition of jazz and despite many attempts to supply a definition or reason for its popularity, the fact remains that jazz can only be played, not talked.

The food at the Jazz and Heritage Festival is as popular as the music. Long lines form at the booths selling Cajun country and Creole specialties, a favorite of which is jambalaya.

The origin of the word "jambalaya" is obscure. One thing, nevertheless, is known—the inspiration for the famous dish came from the bayou country of Louisiana. Jambon à la ya (*jambon* is French for ham and *ya* African for rice) is no longer limited to ham and rice combinations, but includes seafoods of all kinds (shrimp is used most often).

We Kosher-Creole cooks have developed another variation of jambalaya. Taking our clues from the jazz greats, we improvised, brought together seasonings in perfect harmony, and tastefully composed new recipes for those of you who want a jazzed-up version of some of New Orleans' favorite foods.

March

I.

Fish Balls with Encore Sauce
Basin Street Salad
Jazz Jambalaya
Syncopated Succotash
Dixieland Casserole
Sweet Potato Pie

II.

Jazzed-Up Broccoli
Gig Combination Salad
Thousand Island Dressing
Second Liners Jambalaya
Ragtime Yams
Jazzman's Eggplant
Brass Band Bread Pudding

FISH BALLS WITH ENCORE SAUCE

1 32-oz. jar small gefilte-
  fish balls
4 tbsp. yellow mustard
1 tbsp. horseradish
½ cup vinegar
½ cup chopped celery
1 tbsp. paprika

1 cup salad oil
2 tbsp. catsup
½ cup chopped shallots
½ tsp. Tabasco sauce
1 tsp. salt
1 clove garlic, minced
shredded lettuce

Mix all ingredients thoroughly, except fish balls and lettuce. Chill. When ready to serve, line cocktail glasses with lettuce. Place fish balls in glasses and spoon sauce on top. Serves six to eight.

BASIN STREET SALAD

1 lb. fresh okra
2 creole tomatoes, cut into
  bite-size pieces
1 tsp. salt

3 shallots, chopped
¼ cup olive oil
¼ cup tarragon vinegar

Wash okra and remove both ends. Place in saucepan and cover with water. Add salt. Cover and cook on low heat until tender (20 to 30 minutes). Drain and cool.

Combine tomatoes and shallots in salad bowl. Add okra, olive oil, and vinegar. Season with additional salt and pepper to taste. Cover and chill about 2 hours before serving. Serves four to six.

JAZZ JAMBALAYA

1 tbsp. shortening
¼ lb. cubed kosher salami
1 sprig thyme
1 onion, sliced
salt and pepper to taste
2 cups tomatoes
1 cup uncooked rice
1 tbsp. flour

¼ cup minced green pepper
1 bay leaf
1 sprig parsley, minced
1 clove garlic, minced
1 lb. smoked kosher
   sausage
1¼ cups tomato juice

Melt shortening in heavy saucepan over medium heat. Stir in flour, salami, and green pepper. Simmer 5 minutes, stirring constantly.

Add remaining ingredients except rice. Bring to boil. Add rice to liquid. Cover and simmer for 40 minutes until all liquid is absorbed. Serves six.

SYNCOPATED SUCCOTASH

2 cups cooked fresh corn,
   cut from cob
6 slices Beef Frye
1 tbsp. Beef Frye drippings
1 cup tomato sauce

2 cups canned lima beans
liquid from lima beans
1 onion, minced
dash Worcestershire sauce
salt and pepper to taste

Fry Beef Frye until crisp. Remove from pan; reserve drippings. Crumble when cool.

Sauté onion in drippings. Add corn, beans with liquid, tomato sauce, Worcestershire, salt, and pepper. Cook over low heat about 10 to 15 minutes. Stir in crumbled Beef Frye and cook additional 5 minutes. Serves four.

DIXIELAND CASSEROLE

¼ cup olive oil
3 cloves garlic, minced
4 to 5 medium zucchini, cut
   in ¼-inch slices
¼ tsp. oregano
¼ tsp. sweet basil

4 to 5 tomatoes
½ cup seasoned bread
   crumbs
2 tbsp. melted pareve
   margarine

Heat oil in skillet. Add garlic and zucchini, and sauté a few minutes. Remove from heat and set aside.

Peel tomatoes and cut into slices. Place enough zucchini slices in bottom of an oiled 1½-quart casserole to cover bottom. Cover zucchini with tomato slices. Continue to layer zucchini and tomatoes, ending with layer of sliced tomatoes. Sprinkle top of last layer of tomatoes with basil, oregano, and seasoned bread crumbs. Bake uncovered for 30 minutes in 350-degree oven. Serves six.

SWEET POTATO PIE

½ cup sugar
1 tsp. cinnamon
½ tsp. allspice
¼ tsp. mace
½ tsp. salt
1½ cups mashed cooked
   sweet potatoes

2 eggs, slightly beaten
½ cup water
½ cup nondairy creamer
2 tbsp. melted pareve
   margarine
1 9-inch unbaked pie shell

Mix sugar, cinnamon, allspice, mace, and salt. Stir in sweet potatoes. Combine eggs, water, nondairy creamer, and margarine. Add to sweet-potato mixture. Pour into unbaked pie shell. Bake in 400-degree oven about 40 minutes or until set. Test by inserting clean knife in center; if knife comes out clean, filling is set.

JAZZED-UP BROCCOLI

2 10-oz. pkgs. frozen
  broccoli
1 9½-oz. can tuna fish
1 10½-oz. can cream of
  celery soup, undiluted
1 cup seasoned bread
  crumbs

3 tbsp. melted butter or
  margarine
2 cups water
1 egg
cheddar-cheese strips

Mix ingredients together, blending well. Place mixture in ramekins and put cheese strips on top. Bake for about 1 hour at 350°. Sprinkle with additional bread crumbs if desired. Serves six.

GIG COMBINATION SALAD

2 firm heads lettuce
6 creole tomatoes
1 bunch shallots
1 cucumber
1 avocado

1 bunch radishes
few sprigs parsley
salt and pepper to taste
2 green peppers (optional)

Break lettuce in pieces. Cube tomatoes and avocado and dice shallots. Slice cucumber, green peppers, and radishes; add parsley sprigs. Toss all ingredients together in large bowl. Serve with Thousand Island Dressing (see recipe). Serves eight.

THOUSAND ISLAND DRESSING

1 cup mayonnaise
1 clove garlic
catsup
10 or so pimento-stuffed
  olives

2 ribs celery
salt and pepper to taste

Chop olives, garlic, and celery fine. Add mayonnaise and mix well. Pour enough catsup into mixture to make it pink (the more catsup, the sweeter the flavor). Mix well, and store in refrigerator. Salt and pepper to taste. Makes one and a fourth cups.

SECOND LINERS JAMBALAYA

1 1-lb. jar gefilte fish,
  drained
2 cups cooked rice
2 tbsp. butter or pareve
  margarine
¼ cup chopped green
  pepper
½ cup chopped onion

½ tsp. salt
⅛ tsp. pepper
¼ tsp. thyme
1 10½-oz. can condensed
  tomato soup, undiluted
1 cup milk
paprika

Sauté onion and green pepper in butter until tender but not brown. Add salt, pepper, thyme, soup, and milk. Mix with rice. Pour into greased 1½-quart baking dish.

Arrange fish on top; press into rice mixture and sprinkle with paprika. Bake in a 350-degree oven for 30 minutes. Serves four.

RAGTIME YAMS

1 30-oz. can whole yams
¼ cup seedless raisins
juice from 1 lemon
½ cup white sugar
1 tsp. cinnamon
2 tbsp. pareve margarine

1 apple, cored and sliced
2 peaches, peeled and
  sliced
few slices lemon rind
½ cup dark brown sugar

Remove yams and place in casserole dish. Pour liquid from yams into bowl. Add white sugar, brown sugar, and cinnamon, and mix until dissolved. Pour over yams.

Mix fruit together; add to yams and liquid. Dot with margarine. Bake in 400-degree oven about 45 minutes or until syrup has thickened slightly and yams look glazed. (Oranges may be substituted for peaches if desired.) Serves four to five.

JAZZMAN'S EGGPLANT

1 medium eggplant
salt and pepper
flour

1 egg, beaten
bread crumbs
vegetable shortening

Peel and cut eggplant crosswise in ¼-inch slices. Season with salt and pepper. Dip each slice into flour, egg, and then bread crumbs. Fry in a small amount of shortening at 375° until golden brown, turning once. Drain. Serves six.

BRASS BAND BREAD PUDDING

6 slices French bread
  (about ½ inch thick)
4 eggs, separated
pinch salt
1 cup raisins

6 tbsp. sugar
3½ cups milk
1 tbsp. vanilla extract
½ stick butter
1 tsp. cinnamon

Break bread into pieces and soften in small amount of milk; place in 1½-quart baking dish. Beat sugar and egg yolks together until well blended; add milk and mix well. Blend in vanilla, cinnamon, and raisins. Pour mixture over bread. Place dish in pan of water and bake in 300-degree oven for 40 to 50 minutes or until knife comes out clean.

Beat egg whites until foamy. Add salt; gradually add 2 tablespoons sugar and continue beating at high speed until stiff peaks form. Spread whites on top of pudding. Return to oven, raise heat to 350° and bake until meringue is brown. Serves six.

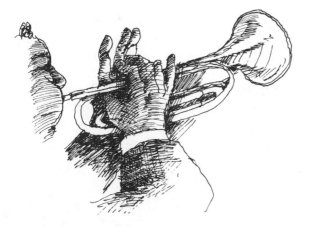

April

מַצָּה

April

Passover à la Spring Fiesta

"The Year's at the Spring
. . . .
God's in His heaven
All's right with the World!"

[Robert Browning, *Pippa Passes I*]

New Orleans loves parades; these festive processions are a must for the beginning of all local celebrations. On the very first Friday after Easter the stately St. Louis Cathedral bells are sounded, officially announcing the commencement of the annual Spring Fiesta.

A queen is crowned at Jackson Square during a colorful coronation pageant. People line the streets of the French Quarter awaiting the Queen and her court as she leads the parade through the streets with floats carrying lovely Southern belles in antebellum dress.

After the parade "A Night in Old New Orleans" is in full swing. There is fun and frolic everywhere. Jackson Square is aglow with lights. Singers can be heard from beautifully decorated balconies, horse-drawn carriages pass, and jazz bands strut by.

During Spring Fiesta there are walking tours through the Vieux Carré, plantation tours, candlelight courtyard tours, riverboat tours, and the eagerly awaited Garden District tours.

Stately mansions in the Garden District—built soon after the Louisiana Purchase in 1803—open their doors. Costumed hostesses (many, direct descendants of the original owners) invite you to stroll through their magnificent landscaped gardens and welcome you inside to view their exquisite antique furnishings and family heirlooms. You will be fascinated as they proudly relate the history of their homes and personal treasures.

To Jewish women in New Orleans, Spring Fiesta invariably means Passover time, when they, too, turn back the hands of time. History and family tradition are the orders of the day. Passover, the eight-day festival commemorating the flight of Jews from Egyptian slavery, is a most joyous holiday. *All* (and we do mean *all*) the family gathers together for the Seder (the Festival Dinner), read from the Haggadah (the book that contains the story of the Exodus), and eat and eat and eat.

Consumption of many everyday foods is forbidden during Passover (products containing leavening, wheat, barley, rice, peas, corn, beans, etc.). We further abstain from our favorite Southern grits. Even permissible foods must bear a certified "Strictly Kosher: May be used for Passover" label.

This is a holiday that calls for traditional recipes with an extra dash here and there of Jewish spices. Notice, though, how discreetly we have blended in a pinch or two of Creole seasoning.

April

Traditional Passover Seder

The Traditional Passover table should be set with a small pitcher of water; a bowl and towel (for ritual washing of hands); wine cups and Haggadahs (booklet containing Seder ceremony and story of Passover) at each place setting; kiddush (wine) cup designated as Elijah's Cup; three matzos (unleavened bread) in sectional matzo cover; and a dish of salt water.

On the symbolic Seder Plate, place the following: roasted shankbone, roasted egg, bitter herbs (usually small pieces of fresh horseradish root or romaine lettuce), sprigs of parsley (to dip in salted water), and horaseth (see recipe).

The candle-lighting ceremony—all blessings to be recited before the Seder begins, together with the meaning and explanation of the symbols on the Seder Plate—can be found in the Traditional Passover Haggadah.

I.

Traditional Seder Menu*

Red Sea Gefilte Fish
Fish Balls
Traditional Chicken Soup
Matzo Balls
Four Sons' Relish Plate
Schnapsy Seder Chicken
Ma Nishtanah Stuffing
Exodus Spicy Squash
Pás-ovér Yam Casserole
Afikomen Asparagus
Pharaoh's Pears
Elijah's Sponge Cake

II.

Kosher Creole Seder Menu*

Chicken Giblet Fricassee
Pesach Onion Soup
Creole Pot Roast Piquant
Galilée Glazed Carrots
Potatoes Dí-Anu
Jaffa Jazzy Beets
Avocado and Grapefruit Salad
Napoleons à la Matzo

*All ingredients listed are available kosher for Passover.

HORASETH

6 apples
3 tbsp. red wine
1 tsp. cinnamon

½ cup ground nuts (pecans or walnuts)

Peel, core, and chop apples until pieces are coarse. Mix with remaining ingredients until well blended. Serves twelve to fifteen.

RED SEA GEFILTE FISH

bones and heads of fish
  (see Fish Balls recipe)
3 cups water

½ tsp. pepper
1 tsp. salt
2 medium onions, quartered

Fillet fish and reserve back and head bones, discarding skin. Combine bones, water, salt, pepper, and onions. Cover and simmer for 10 minutes. Add Fish Balls (see recipe).

FISH BALLS

1½ lbs. redfish fillets
1 lb. trout or whitefish fillets
1 egg, beaten
¾ tsp. pepper

1 medium onion, grated
1 carrot, grated
1 tbsp. matzo meal
2 tsp. salt

Grind fish fillets once with fine blade. Add matzo meal, onion, carrot, egg, and salt and pepper. Mix thoroughly, adding just a little water if necessary to make mixture moist. Wet hands and form fish into 8 balls (not too tightly packed).

Simmer in stock for 1¾ hours. After 1 hour taste to see if stock has enough seasoning. Adjust if necessary. Makes eight large balls.

TRADITIONAL CHICKEN SOUP

1 6-lb. pullet with giblets
2½ qts. water
1 onion
3 stalks celery

8 sprigs parsley
2 carrots
1 celery root
salt and pepper

Clean and wash chicken thoroughly and scrape giblets. Combine chicken, giblets, water, and onion in a saucepan. Bring to a boil and skim surface of broth. Cover and cook over medium heat for 1 hour.

Add celery, parsley, carrots, celery root, salt, and pepper. Cook over low heat for 1½ hours longer or until chicken is tender. Strain soup and serve with any desired garnish. Serves six to eight.

MATZO BALLS

3 eggs, separated
⅓ cup melted schmaltz
1 tbsp. hot water

¾ cup matzo meal
salt to taste

Beat egg yolks until well blended; add hot water and beat again. Add schmaltz and beat; add matzo meal and beat. Fold in stiffly beaten egg whites and pinch of salt. Let stand in refrigerator until firm.

With oiled hands, shape into balls about size of a walnut and drop in boiling salt water. Cover and cook 30 to 45 minutes. Makes about twelve to fifteen balls.

FOUR SONS' RELISH PLATE

On large sectional relish dish, place pickled sauerkraut, Passover dill tomato sections, pickled beet slices, and sweet and sour cucumber spears.

Keep chilled until ready to serve.

SCHNAPSY SEDER CHICKEN

2 frying chickens, cut up
½ cup peanut oil
2½ tsp. salt
2 tsp. paprika
1½ tsp. pepper
1 tsp. onion powder
½ tsp. garlic powder
2 cubes chicken bouillon,
    crushed

1 10½-oz. can tomato sauce
    with mushrooms
3 ripe creole tomatoes,
    chopped
2 large onions, sliced
5 medium zucchini, sliced
1½ cups Passover red wine

Heat oil in Dutch oven over medium heat. Add chicken pieces and brown well on all sides. Sprinkle in salt, paprika, pepper, onion powder, garlic powder, and bouillon cubes.

Reduce heat to medium low; add chopped tomatoes and tomato and mushroom sauce, onion, zucchini, and wine. Cook covered 30 minutes. Uncover and continue cooking another 15 minutes or until liquid is somewhat reduced and chicken is done. Serves eight.

MA NISHTANAH STUFFING

¾ cup vegetable shortening
    or chicken fat
¾ cup minced onion
10 matzos, finely broken
1 tsp. salt
¼ tsp. pepper

½ tsp. garlic powder
1 tbsp. paprika
1 egg
1½ cans (2 cups) condensed
    clear chicken soup,
    undiluted

Sauté onion in fat until tender but not browned. Add broken matzos and toast lightly. Combine salt, pepper, garlic powder, paprika, egg, and soup. Add to matzo mixture. (For a variation, add chopped pecans or walnuts, mushrooms, or giblets and chicken livers to stuffing.) Makes enough to stuff a ten- to twelve-pound bird.

NOTE: This makes a dry stuffing. If you prefer a moister stuffing, increase the condensed chicken soup to 2 cans.

EXODUS SPICY SQUASH

2½ to 3 lbs. squash
boiling salted water
¼ cup peanut oil (kosher for
    Passover)

½ cup chopped onion
2 tbsp. sugar
1½ tsp. grated orange peel
1 tsp. cinnamon

Wash squash; peel and remove seeds and fibers. Cut into pieces and cook in small amount of boiling salted water until tender (about 15 to 20 minutes). Drain well and mash thoroughly.

Heat peanut oil and sauté onion until tender. Combine sautéed onion, mashed squash, sugar, orange peel, and cinnamon. Blend well and pour into greased 1-quart casserole. Bake uncovered in 350-degree oven for 20 minutes. Serves four.

PÁS-OVÉR YAM CASSEROLE

6 medium sweet potatoes
    (about 3 lbs.)
2 cups applesauce
¾ tsp. cinnamon

¾ cup honey
3 tbsp. melted chicken fat
    or pareve margarine

Cook, peel, and slice sweet potatoes. Mix applesauce and cinnamon. In a greased 2-quart baking dish, arrange alternate layers of sweet-potato slices and applesauce, drizzling honey and fat over each layer. Bake uncovered in a 350-degree oven for 45 minutes, basting occasionally. Serves six to eight.

AFIKOMEN ASPARAGUS

2 lbs. fresh asparagus, or
  2 15-oz. cans whole
  asparagus
2 10½-oz. cans condensed
  pareve Passover
  mushroom soup,
  undiluted

4 hard-cooked eggs, sliced
½ cup sliced almonds
½ cup sliced cooked
  mushrooms

Wash fresh asparagus and trim ends of stems. Divide and tie asparagus together, making 2 bundles. In large kettle, place bundles upright with stems down in enough boiling water to cover stems. Cook about 10 minutes or until stems are tender. Turn bundles over so that tips are covered with water and cook additional 5 minutes. Remove and untie bundles.

In casserole dish, layer asparagus, soup, eggs, almonds, and mushrooms; continue layering, ending with almonds and mushrooms. Bake in preheated 350-degree oven for 45 minutes. Serves six to eight.

PHARAOH'S PEARS

½ cup sugar
2 cups water
1½ tsp. cinnamon
1 tbsp. lemon juice

8 whole medium pears,
  peeled
1 cup Passover red wine

Mix sugar, water, cinnamon, and lemon juice in pan. Poach pears in this syrup until tender (about 25 minutes). Add wine and cook 10 to 15 minutes longer until pears become wine colored. Remove fruit to serving bowl and cook liquid until reduced by ⅓.

Place pears on slices of Passover sponge cake and dribble warm syrup on top. Serves four.

ELIJAH'S SPONGE CAKE

9 eggs, separated
2 cups sugar
juice and grated rind of 1
   lemon
pinch salt

¾ cup Passover potato
   starch
¾ cup Passover cake meal
6 tbsp. hot water

Beat egg yolks, sugar, lemon juice, and lemon rind with mixer until thick and lemon colored (about 10 minutes at medium speed). Add salt to potato starch and cake meal. Add water and cake meal alternately to yolks, continuing to beat until well blended.

Beat egg whites until stiff and carefully fold into batter. Pour batter into ungreased tube pan and bake in preheated 350-degree oven about 50 minutes or until straw inserted into center of cake comes out clean. When done, invert pan and allow to cool before removing cake.

CHICKEN GIBLET FRICASSEE

giblets and necks from 3
   chickens
3 medium onions, diced
2 lbs. ground beef
2 eggs, slightly beaten
2 matzos, finely broken

⅔ cup cold water
2 tsp. salt
¼ tsp. pepper
2 tsp. paprika
1 10½-oz. can tomato sauce
   with mushrooms

Cut giblets into small pieces and break necks in half. Add diced onion and cover with water. Cover and simmer until tender (about 1½ to 2 hours). Soak broken matzos in cold water and combine with ground beef and beaten eggs. Shape into small meatballs and drop into hot giblet mixture.

Add seasonings and tomato and mushroom sauce; cover and cook gently for at least ½ hour. Serves four to six.

PESACH ONION SOUP

1½ tbsp. chicken fat
3 cups onion, sliced paper
   thin

4 cups strained chicken
   broth
salt and pepper to taste

In a 3-quart saucepan, sauté onion in chicken fat over low heat until soft and golden brown. Add chicken broth. Bring to a boil, cover; reduce heat and simmer for about 30 to 40 minutes. Serve with Passover soup nuts if desired. Serves five to six.

CREOLE POT ROAST PIQUANT

3- to 4-lb. pot roast
¼ cup potato starch
2 tsp. salt
¼ tsp. pepper
2 tbsp. peanut oil
1 cup chopped ripe creole
   tomatoes

2 onions, halved and sliced
¼ tsp. ginger
1 cup orange juice
½ cup Passover red wine

Coat meat with mixture of potato starch, salt, and pepper. Brown on both sides in hot oil.

Add tomatoes and onions. Cover and simmer 2 hours. Add orange juice, wine, and ginger; cover and continue to simmer 1 hour longer or until meat is tender. Serves eight.

GALILÉE GLAZED CARROTS

12 to 14 large carrots
4 tbsp. melted pareve
    margarine

4 tbsp. honey
juice and rind of 1 orange
¼ tsp. cinnamon

Peel carrots and cook in boiling, salted water until tender; drain. Mix margarine, honey, and cinnamon together. When well blended, add carrots, orange juice, and rind. Cook until glazed, carefully turning while cooking. Serves six.

POTATOES DÍ-ANU

3 lbs. new potatoes (about
    18)
2 tsp. salt
½ cup pareve margarine

⅛ tsp. pepper
1 10½-oz. can condensed
    Passover mushroom
    soup, undiluted

Pare potatoes and place in cold water until ready to use; drain and place in saucepan. Cover with water and add salt. Bring to a boil, cover, and simmer 10 minutes.

Drain thoroughly. Melt margarine in large, heavy skillet. Place potatoes in pan and sprinkle with pepper. Cover tightly and cook over low heat 10 minutes or until browned on one side. Turn, cover, and cook 10 minutes longer. Add soup, cover, and simmer 10 minutes or until tender. Serves six to eight.

JAFFA JAZZY BEETS

2 bunches beets, peeled
and sliced thin
2 medium apples, sliced
thin
2 oranges, peeled and cut
into segments
¼ cup white raisins

¼ tsp. cinnamon
1 cup orange juice
2 tbsp. peanut oil
1 tbsp. honey
1 tsp. salt
½ tsp. grated orange peel

Arrange alternate layers of beets, apples, and orange segments in 1½-quart casserole dish. Sprinkle with cinnamon. Combine orange juice, oil, honey, salt, and grated orange peel; pour over beets. Top with raisins.

Cover and bake in a 425-degree oven for 1 hour or until tender. Serves six to eight.

AVOCADO AND GRAPEFRUIT SALAD

2 ripe avocados
2 grapefruit
lemon juice
3 strips kosher Beef Frye

½ cup prepared Passover
mayonnaise (or Passover
French dressing)
4 to 6 romaine leaves

Cut avocados in half, remove seeds, and peel; then cut into wedges. Brush lemon juice on cut surfaces. Halve grapefruit, remove seeds and rind, and cut into segments. Fry Beef Frye in skillet until crisp. Drain and crumble.

Toss all ingredients together with mayonnaise or French dressing. Serve on romaine leaves. Serves four to six.

NAPOLEONS À LA MATZO

6 apples
6 thin tea matzos
6 tbsp. sugar
1 tsp. salt
1½ tsp. cinnamon

2 egg whites
2 tbsp. sugar
1 pkg. Passover lemon
   custard mix

Pare and slice apples. Dip matzos in water just long enough to soften. Place a layer of matzos in bottom of a greased baking dish and cover with layer of apples. Combine sugar, salt, and cinnamon. Sprinkle ⅓ of sugar mixture over apples. Place another layer of apples over sugar mixture and sprinkle again with ⅓ of sugar mixture. Repeat until all apples and sugar are used, ending with layer of apples. Place dish in pan of water and bake in 350-degree oven until apples are done (about 45 minutes).

Beat egg whites until stiff, gradually adding 2 tablespoons sugar. Spread on top of apples and return to oven to brown. Cut into squares when cool.

Prepare lemon custard according to directions on package. Just before serving, pour custard on top of squares. Serves eight to ten.

April

Spring Fiesta Menus

I.

Carriage Trade Chicken Livers
Candlelight Soup
Chicken Clemenceau
Jackson Square Salad
Garden District Parfait
Courtyard Crunch

II.

Fiesta Fish Hors D'Oeuvres
Horseradish Dip
Spring Salmon Étouffée
Vieux Carré Veal Birds
Louisiana Rice Dressing
Rebel Green Beans Piquant
Monsieur's Mushrooms in Wine
Antebellum Brandied Peaches
Madame's Marinated Salad
Meringues Aux Fruits

CARRIAGE TRADE CHICKEN LIVERS

12 chicken livers
salt and pepper to taste
12 slices Beef Frye

Rinse chicken livers, remove any fatty tissue, and pat dry. Wrap each liver in 1 slice Beef Frye and fasten with toothpick. Season, being careful not to use too much salt as Beef Frye is already salted.

Place in flat roasting pan and broil on both sides until Beef Frye is crisp and livers are done. Delicious served on toast with smothered onion slices. Serves three to four.

CANDLELIGHT SOUP

3 6½-oz. cans tuna in oil
oil from tuna
1 cup sliced celery
1 cup chopped green pepper
3 onions, chopped

1 10-oz. can pareve
mushroom soup
3 cups water
1 tsp. salt
¼ tsp. pepper

Drain oil from tuna and heat in large saucepan. Add celery, green pepper, and onion and cook over medium heat, stirring occasionally, until celery is tender.

Separate tuna into large pieces. Add tuna and remaining ingredients and mix well. Cover and simmer for about 5 minutes. Serves eight.

CHICKEN CLEMENCEAU

1 frying chicken, cut into
  8 pieces
2 tbsp. flour
1 17-oz. can petit pois peas
1 4-oz. can whole
  mushrooms
salt and pepper
dash Tabasco sauce
1 chicken bouillon cube

½ cup pareve margarine
1 tbsp. grated onion or 1
  shallot, finely chopped
2 large potatoes
1 tbsp. parsley, chopped fine
1 tbsp. Worcestershire
  sauce
1 cup warm water
½ cup sherry or white wine

Drain peas and mushrooms, reserving liquid from both. Sprinkle chicken with salt and pepper; brown in margarine and remove from skillet. Add flour and onion to drippings, and brown over low heat. Add liquid from peas and mushrooms to onions and stir thoroughly. Add chicken. Cover and simmer until chicken is tender (about 45 minutes).

Peel potatoes and cut into 1-inch cubes; fry in deep fat until golden brown. Drain on absorbent paper.

Dissolve bouillon cube in warm water. Add peas, mushrooms, parsley, salt, pepper, Worcestershire sauce, Tabasco sauce, and bouillon to chicken; simmer 10 minutes. Stir in wine and potatoes; heat additional 2 minutes and serve. Serves four to five.

JACKSON SQUARE SALAD

1 avocado
2 slices lox, diced
2 tsp. finely chopped celery
3 pickled onions

2 pimento-stuffed olives,
  minced
½ tsp. Worcestershire sauce
lettuce

Cut avocado in half. Remove seed and pulp. Mash pulp and mix with lox, onions, celery, stuffed olives, and Worcestershire sauce. Place on bed of lettuce. Serves four.

GARDEN DISTRICT PARFAIT

3 cups sponge cake, cut into
½-inch cubes
¼ cup sweet red wine

1 cup drained fruit cocktail
1 cup nondairy whipped
topping

Arrange alternate layers of cake cubes, fruit cocktail, and whipped topping in parfait or sherbet glasses. Sprinkle each cake layer generously with wine. Chill and serve. Serves six.

COURTYARD CRUNCH

6 bananas, peeled
2 tbsp. melted pareve
margarine
½ cup Concord grape wine

juice of 1 lime
2 tbsp. brown sugar
¼ tsp. cinnamon
½ cup chopped pecans

Slice bananas lengthwise. Place in shallow 10- by 14-inch pan. Mix all other ingredients together, except pecans. Pour mixture over bananas. Bake under broiler, basting until bananas are light brown. Remove from broiler, sprinkle with chopped pecans, and serve while still hot. Serves six.

FIESTA FISH HORS D'OEUVRES

1 16-oz. jar small gefilte-
fish balls
½ cup matzo meal
peanut oil (enough to
measure 1 inch deep in
pan)

Horseradish Dip (see recipe)

Heat peanut oil to 375° in a deep, straight-sided pot. Drain fish balls and roll in matzo meal; place in a wire basket or strainer and fry until golden brown. Serve hot with Horseradish Dip (see recipe). Serves four.

HORSERADISH DIP

¼ cup mayonnaise
¼ cup prepared red
  horseradish

Mix together and serve in a bowl.

SPRING SALMON ÉTOUFFÉE

2 15½-oz. cans salmon
6 tbsp. pareve margarine
2 tbsp. flour
1¼ cups chopped onions
1 tsp. tomato purée
1 clove garlic, chopped
2 shallots, chopped

¼ tsp. Tabasco sauce
¼ tsp. pepper
½ tsp. salt
¼ cup chopped parsley
1 cup water
½ cup chopped celery

Melt margarine in pan and remove from heat. Stir in flour until smooth. Return to heat and cook until dark brown, stirring constantly. Lower heat; stir in onions, shallots, garlic, and celery and cook until soft (10 to 15 minutes), stirring often.

Lower heat to simmer. Dissolve tomato purée in ¼ cup water and stir into roux. Add remaining water, salmon, and parsley. Stir to blend. Add Tabasco sauce, salt, and pepper. Cover and simmer about 20 minutes.

Serve over bed of hot rice. Serves ten to twelve.

VIEUX CARRÉ VEAL BIRDS

8 veal cutlets, cut thin
salt and pepper
1 tbsp. Worcestershire
  sauce
8 tbsp. Louisiana Rice
  Dressing (see recipe)

flour
¼ tsp. oregano
1 tbsp. onion soup mix

Pound veal cutlets with a mallet until thin, being careful not to split meat. Season with salt and pepper.

Lay squares of veal on a flat surface; put a spoonful of dressing in center of each one. Roll up squares and secure with toothpicks. Roll in flour and brown in hot fat.

Add ½ cup cold water and cover tightly so that steam will not escape. Cook 1½ hours until brown.

Make gravy by adding Worcestershire sauce, onion soup, and oregano. Serves four.

LOUISIANA RICE DRESSING

½ lb. broiled chicken
  livers, ground
3 cooked chicken giblets,
  ground
2 large onions, ground
2 cloves garlic, ground
1 cup ground celery

½ cup minced parsley
½ cup ground shallots
6 tbsp. pareve margarine
1 egg, well beaten
4 cups cooked rice
salt, pepper, and cayenne to
  taste

Sauté livers, giblets, onions, garlic, celery, and shallots in margarine until onions and celery are soft and meat is brown. Add egg, parsley, salt, pepper, and cayenne to taste; stir. Cover and simmer 10 minutes. Add cooked rice, mix thoroughly, and heat through. Yields enough dressing for 10- to 12-pound turkey, or may be baked in greased casserole dish in 350-degree oven 20 minutes. Serves eight to ten.

NOTE: The secret of this recipe is that meat and vegetables are ground, not chopped.

REBEL GREEN BEANS PIQUANT

1 lb. whole fresh green
  beans
1 cup water
4 slices Beef Frye
2 tsp. sugar
¼ tsp. salt

1 medium onion, thinly
  sliced
½ tsp. salt
3 tbsp. red wine vinegar
1 tsp. Worcestershire sauce

In saucepan combine green beans, onion, water, and ½ teaspoon salt. Cook, covered, 25 minutes or until beans are tender; drain.

In skillet cook Beef Frye until crisp. Drain, reserving about 3 tablespoons Beef Frye drippings. Crumble Beef Frye and set aside.

Return reserved drippings to skillet; stir in vinegar, sugar, Worcestershire sauce, and ¼ teaspoon salt. Bring mixture to boiling. Pour sauce over beans in saucepan, sprinkle with crumbled Beef Frye, and toss lightly to mix. Cover, return to heat for 2 to 3 minutes to heat through and blend flavors. Serves six.

MONSIEUR'S MUSHROOMS IN WINE

1 lb. cleaned, chopped
  mushrooms
3 tbsp. vegetable oil
½ tsp. salt

dash thyme
1 bay leaf
dash white pepper
⅓ cup dry red wine

Brown mushrooms in a saucepan in vegetable oil with salt, pepper, thyme, and bay leaf. Add the wine. Cover and cook over low heat about 5 minutes. Remove bay leaf before serving. Serves four.

ANTEBELLUM BRANDIED PEACHES

4 lbs. peaches   1½ cups water
6 cups sugar   brandy

Remove skin from peaches. Bring sugar and water to boil and boil for 5 minutes. Place peaches in syrup and simmer gently until fruit is easily pierced but not soft. Remove peaches from syrup and drain.

Boil syrup rapidly until it thickens (about 10 minutes). Pour syrup over peaches and allow to stand until cool. Lift the fruit from syrup and placed in hot, sterilized jars. Measure syrup and add an equal amount of brandy. Pour over fruit in the jars and seal. Makes two quarts.

MADAME'S MARINATED SALAD

1 large cucumber, sliced   ½ tsp. Seasonall
1 14-oz. can artichoke   1 tsp. sugar
  hearts   ½ cup tarragon vinegar
1 tsp. salt   3 tbsp. olive oil
¼ tsp. garlic powder   ¼ tsp. onion powder
1 red onion, thinly sliced

Mix ingredients except cucumber, artichokes, and onions. Pour dressing over vegetables and marinate in refrigerator for 4 to 6 hours or overnight. Serves four.

MERINGUES AUX FRUITS

4 egg whites
½ cup finely chopped
  pecans
a little pareve margarine
2 cups assorted fresh fruit

1 cup sugar
pinch cream of tartar
a little flour
4 tbsp. grenadine syrup

To make the shells, beat egg whites until frothy. Add cream of tartar and continue beating until firm peaks form. Add sugar gradually, about 2 tablespoons at a time, and continue beating until sugar is completely dissolved and meringue is very stiff and shiny.

Grease 12 small tart pans lightly and dust with flour. Spoon in meringue and spread evenly in the pans with the back of a spoon. Sprinkle with chopped nuts and bake at 200° for about 2 hours until crisp. (The meringue must not rise; just dry out. You may have to prop open the oven door if it starts to brown.) Remove from pans and cool.

Prepare fruit by slicing it into even pieces. Drizzle with grenadine and refrigerate until serving time. Spoon into shells and serve. Makes about twelve small tarts.

May

May

Magnolia Blossom Buffets

The official state flower of Louisiana is the magnolia, named after the French botanist Pierre Magnol (1638-1750). Suspended from dark olive leaves, the magnolia's creamy white petals reach six to twelve inches in length. When its fragrance fills the air, everyone knows the magnolia is in full bloom. Magnolia trees often rise to heights of 100 feet, and their spreading limbs provide welcome shade in summer. As the flower matures, a conelike fruit about the size of an egg appears, which ripens to a reddish color. Botanists claim the tree is one of the most ancient; its ancestors thrived in the swamps of early times.

Louisiana's state flower attracts everyone with an eye for beauty. Artists in Jackson Square sketch it as one of their favorite still-life subjects. Visitors click their cameras, capturing on film every detail.

The sprawling magnolia trees in uptown New Orleans were planted by the Americans who were rejected by the Creoles and forced to build their homes outside the Old Quarter. They settled in today's very fashionable Garden District. Their homes were large, stately mansions. Unlike the Creole cottages with hidden patios that rose from the banquette (sidewalk), the uptown gardens were in full view. These homes were set back from the street, almost hidden behind the magnificent magnolia trees interspersed with palms and live oaks.

Your own shady patio or beautiful garden is the perfect setting for serving these tasty, cool, and tempting recipes.

May

I.

Gin Fizz
Spicy Cheese Crisps
Magnolia Salad
Creamy Mayonnaise Dressing
Banana Fritters
Southern Broccoli Nut Ring
Crescent City Cheese Bread
New Orleans Frozen Cream Cheese

II.

Avocado Creosher Canapés
Magnolia Melon Balls
Nanny's Stuffed Peppers
Southern Blintz Soufflé
Pain Perdu
Patio Peach Jam
Pierre's Strawberry Jam
Cherries Jubilee

GIN FIZZ

4 tsp. sugar
4 oz. cream
4 egg whites
2 oz. orange juice

2 oz. lemon juice
2 oz. lime juice
8 oz. gin

Blend with ice in a large shaker until smooth. Serves four.

SPICY CHEESE CRISPS

2 sticks margarine, softened
2 cups Rice Krispies
2 tsp. Seasonall
few drops Tabasco sauce

2 cups sifted flour
2 cups grated sharp cheddar
  cheese (about ½ lb.)
2 tsp. red pepper

Cream margarine with Seasonall, Tabasco, and pepper. Add cheese and flour and blend well. Fold in Rice Krispies. Roll into small balls and place on ungreased cookie sheets about 2 inches apart. Flatten balls with fork. Bake in 400-degree oven 10 to 12 minutes, until edges brown. Do not over brown, as this will produce a slightly bitter taste. Remove from cookie sheet when cool. Makes about eight dozen crisps.

KOSHER CREOLE COOKBOOK

MAGNOLIA SALAD

1 16-oz. can of salmon,
 drained
1 small head romaine
 lettuce
1 small head escarole
1 small head Bibb or Boston
 lettuce

4 hard-cooked eggs
2 large tomatoes
1 cucumber, sliced
1 small onion, sliced
parsley or watercress for
 garnish

Rinse salad greens, separate leaves, and spin or pat dry. Line 4 individual salad bowls or 1 large salad bowl with greens. Arrange wedges of egg, tomato, cucumber slices, and large chunks of salmon on the greens and top with onion slices or garnish with parsley leaves or watercress. Serve with Creamy Mayonnaise Dressing (see recipe). Serves four.

CREAMY MAYONNAISE DRESSING

1 egg yolk
¾ cup oil
juice from ½ lemon

1 tsp. Creole mustard or ¼
 tsp. dry mustard
salt and pepper to taste

Place egg yolk in a bowl. Add mustard and a pinch of salt and beat until slightly thickened. Add oil drop by drop. When mixture has become very thick, add a little lemon juice, then rest of oil, drop by drop. Continue beating until thick and creamy. Add salt and pepper to taste. Makes about one cup.

BANANA FRITTERS

2 cups sifted enriched
   flour
1 tsp. salt
½ cup finely chopped
   almonds (or pecans)
1 egg, beaten
4 firm bananas, peeled and
   cut into 1½-inch pieces

⅓ cup sugar
1 tbsp. baking powder
½ tsp. ground cardamom
1 to 1¼ cups milk
oil for deep frying
½ cup granulated sugar

Sift together flour, sugar, baking powder, salt, and cardamom into mixing bowl. Stir in nuts. Blend together egg and 1 cup milk. Add liquid all at once to flour mixture, stirring until well blended. If necessary, stir in more milk to make a medium-thick batter.

Dip banana pieces into batter one at a time, turning to coat completely. Fry in preheated 375-degree fat until golden brown, turning once. Drain thoroughly on absorbent paper.

Measure ½ cup sugar into brown paper bag. Add fritters, 1 or 2 at a time, and shake gently to coat completely. Serve warm. Makes about twenty fritters.

SOUTHERN BROCCOLI NUT RING

3 eggs
2 10-oz. pkgs. frozen
   chopped broccoli
½ cup bread crumbs
¾ cup chopped pecans
¼ cup vegetable oil

¼ tsp. salt
⅛ tsp. ginger
12 small new potatoes
2 tbsp. butter
¼ cup chopped pimento

Cook broccoli according to directions on package and drain. Beat eggs; add drained broccoli and all other ingredients except potatoes, butter, and pimento. Pour mixture into greased ring mold. Bake in preheated 350-degree oven for 25 minutes or until firm.

Pare potatoes and boil in slightly salted water until done. Remove potatoes and add butter and pimento. Turn out mold onto hot platter and fill center with potatoes. Serves six.

CRESCENT CITY CHEESE BREAD

1½ cups milk
4 tsp. butter
½ cup warm water
1 egg, well beaten
6 cups sifted flour
⅓ cup sugar

1 tbsp. salt
2 pkgs. dry yeast
1½ cups grated sharp
   cheddar cheese
melted butter

Scald milk in saucepan. Stir in sugar, butter, and salt. Cool milk mixture until lukewarm. While milk mixture cools, put warm water into a large bowl. Sprinkle yeast over water and stir until dissolved. Stir in milk mixture, egg, and cheese.

Add 3 cups flour; beat until smooth. Stir in enough additional flour so dough no longer sticks to sides of bowl (about 3 to 3½ cups). Place dough on a lightly floured board and knead about 10 minutes, or until smooth and elastic.

Divide dough in half and shape into loaves. Place in two buttered 9- by 5- by 3-inch loaf pans. If desired, brush tops lightly with melted butter. Cover with a towel and let rise in a warm place free from drafts until loaves have doubled in bulk (about 30 minutes).

Bake in 375-degree oven for 30 to 35 minutes. Remove bread from pan at once, and cool on wire rack. Makes two loaves.

NEW ORLEANS FROZEN CREAM CHEESE

2 11-oz. cartons of
  creamed Creole cheese
  with cream*
1 cup evaporated milk

1 cup sugar
½ tsp. vanilla extract
1 egg white, beaten until
  stiff

Mash cream cheese through colander so as to keep mixture smooth. Blend creamed cheese and cream with evaporated milk. Add sugar and vanilla. Fold in egg white. Pour into ice cube tray and freeze. Serves six.

*NOTE: Creamed Creole Cheese can be purchased only in New Orleans and immediate surrounding areas. For those living outside New Orleans, this creamed cheese can be made with the following ingredients:

1 12-oz. carton dry curd
4 oz. heavy whipping cream
4 oz. half-and-half cream

Combine all three ingredients. This will yield the equivalent of 2 11-oz. cartons of creamed Creole cheese with cream. Proceed with other ingredients and recipe directions.

AVOCADO CREOSHER CANAPES

2 ripe avocados
½ cup mayonnaise
3 tbsp. lemon juice
1 tsp. chili powder

¼ tsp. garlic powder
¼ tsp. Tabasco sauce
¼ tsp. salt

Slice avocado and remove seed. Scoop out pulp and mash very fine, or blend in blender until smooth. Stir in remaining ingredients, mixing well. Refrigerate for 1½ hours before serving. Serve as dip with raw vegetables or as spread with slices of party rye. Makes enough spread for about twenty-five slices of party rye.

MAGNOLIA MELON BALLS

3 honeydew melons
1 cup watermelon balls
1 cup cantaloupe balls
1 cup honeydew melon balls

1 cup drained pineapple
  chunks
1 cup sliced bananas
½ cup Sabra liqueur

Cut 1 inch off top of each melon and scoop out seeds. Combine fruit and place in melon cavities. Pour ½ cup liqueur over fruit in each melon and replace tops. Chill for 2 hours or more. Cut melons in half to serve. Serves six.

NANNY'S STUFFED PEPPERS

1½ sticks butter or pareve
  margarine
1 cup chopped celery
1 bay leaf
1 tbsp. parsley
½ loaf stale French bread
½ tsp. Tabasco sauce
5 medium bell peppers,
  halved

2 large onions, minced
1 bell pepper, minced
2 cloves garlic, minced
½ tsp. thyme
2 6½-oz. cans tuna
1½ tsp. salt
1 egg

Sauté onions, minced bell pepper, celery, and garlic in butter or margarine until light brown. Add bay leaf, thyme, parsley, tuna, and French bread that has been soaked in water until soft and squeezed out. Add salt and Tabasco and blend thoroughly. Remove from heat; add egg and blend. Remove seeds and membrane from bell pepper halves and cook in boiling salted water about 5 minutes; drain.

Pile tuna mixture into pepper shells and bake in a 350-degree oven 15 to 20 minutes or until heated through. Makes ten stuffed pepper halves or about five servings.

SOUTHERN BLINTZE SOUFFLÉ

12 frozen cheese blintzes,
  defrosted
¼ lb. butter
4 eggs, well beaten

1½ cups sour cream
¼ cup sugar
½ tsp. salt
1 tsp. vanilla extract

Melt butter in 2-quart casserole; place blintzes in casserole in 1 layer. Blend other ingredients with well-beaten eggs and pour over blintzes. Bake 45 minutes in 350-degree oven until top starts to brown. Serve with fruit topping or sour cream. Serves eight.

PAIN PERDU

3 tbsp. sugar
⅛ tsp. salt
2 eggs, beaten
2 tbsp. butter

½ cup milk
¼ tsp. vanilla extract
6 slices stale bread
sugar, honey, or jam

Combine sugar, milk, salt, vanilla, and eggs; beat well. Soak bread in mixture; fry in hot butter until well browned on both sides. Sprinkle with sugar or pour honey or jam on top. Serves six.

PATIO PEACH JAM

2 lbs. peaches
1½ lbs. sugar

Scald, peel, and pit peaches and cut into quarters. Crush layer of fruit in kettle, cover with sugar, and continue in alternate layers until all is used. Let stand several hours; then heat slowly until sugar dissolves completely, stirring occasionally.

Bring to a boil and cook, stirring frequently, until fruit is clear and somewhat thickened. Pour into 2 hot, sterilized pint jars and seal. Makes 2 pints.

PIERRE'S STRAWBERRY JAM

4 cups cleaned strawberries
5 cups sugar
½ cup lemon juice

Put berries into a large saucepan, sprinkle sugar over them, and let stand 4 to 5 hours. Then place over low heat and bring to a boil. Let boil 8 minutes; add lemon juice and cook 2 minutes longer.

Cool in pan; skim and shake occasionally so that fruit settles. Pour into 2 hot, sterilized pint jars and seal. Makes 2 pints.

CHERRIES JUBILEE

1 16-oz. jar pitted
  cherries
liquid from cherries
¼ cup sugar

1 tbsp. cornstarch
1¼ cup brandy
1 qt. vanilla ice cream

Place cherries with juice, sugar, and cornstarch in saucepan. Cook over low heat until slightly thick (about 5 minutes). Remove from heat, pour into silver bowl, and stir in 1 cup brandy. In ladle, ignite ¼ cup brandy and lower into mixture in bowl, ladling mixture as it flames. When flame dies down, spoon cherry mixture over ice cream and serve immediately. Serves six.

June

June

Plantation Pic-noshes

As early as the 1700s great plantations, ranging in size from 500 to 1,000 acres, lined the river road. The grounds stretched to the banks of the Mississippi River where barges were laden with unparalleled crops of cotton, sugar cane, indigo, rice, and tobacco to be shipped to faraway ports.

By the mid 1800s, more than half of America's millionaires had amassed enormous wealth from the productive soil of the Mississippi Valley. Theirs were the fortunes that built the opulent plantations that by this time stretched along both sides of the river as far north as Natchez, Mississippi.

Plantation life was one of the most important times in Louisiana history. Colonial archives reveal that some plantations were parts of land grants and date back to the late eighteenth century. However, plantations reached their golden years in the nineteenth century when these elegant mansions and formal gardens along the river roads gave rise to the great River Road era.

Many Greek-Revival plantation homes had galleries encircling the second story, surrounded by sprawling lawns, majestic trees, and formal *parterres* (flower beds). Often bedrooms were downstairs and the upper floors were given over to a ballroom, dining room, and nursery. The kitchen, slave quarters, smokehouses, carriage house, tool sheds, stables, and barn were behind the house. Farther back the grounds served as a family cemetery.

Elegant furnishings were imported from France, Italy, and England; and other furniture was hand carved by expert craftsmen in New Orleans. The interior splendor was the setting for the parties, dances, and musicals; outdoors the landed gentry pursued their favorite sports—hunting the hounds and horse racing.

Here, within these settings, African and West Indies cooks brought Creole cooking into its own. They were delighted when the month of June arrived, for they knew they would soon be called upon to show and serve their specialties at plantation picnics.

Something was missing, though, at those plantation picnics—noshes (a tempting snack, or sampling of food). But you'll find them in a wicker basket if it's packed with our Kosher Creole plantation pic-noshes.

June

Pickled Cauliflower
Pickled String Beans
Watermelon Pickles
"Pic-Nosh" Potato Salad
Poor Boy Sandwiches
Cajun Kebobs
Plantation Chicken
Creole Bar-B-Q Sauce
Short Ribs with Nosher's Bar-B-Q Sauce
Country Side Bar-B-Q'd Hot Dogs
Glazed Picnic "Sham"
Cotton-Pickin' Eggs
Calas Muffins
Deep Delta Peach Pie
Bandana Bread
Gallery Glazed Strawberry Pie

PICKLED CAULIFLOWER

4 lbs. cauliflower (2 large
 heads)
4 cups white vinegar
2 cups sugar
1 tbsp. whole cloves
1 tbsp. whole allspice

2 tsp. mustard seed
4 bay leaves
2 sticks cinnamon
1 gal. brine (2 cups coarse
 salt added to 1 gal. water)

Wash cauliflower and separate into flowerets. Place cauliflower pieces in brine and allow to soak for 1 hour.

Stir sugar and vinegar together. Tie cloves, allspice, mustard seeds, bay leaves, and cinnamon in cheesecloth. Add to sugar mixture and bring to a boil over medium fire. Continue boiling additional 3 to 5 minutes. Drain cauliflower pieces from brine and add to sugar mixture. Bring to a boil and continue cooking additional 3 to 4 minutes. Place in 4 sterilized pint jars. Cover with liquid and seal. Makes four pints.

PICKLED STRING BEANS

2 lbs. tender string beans
1 tsp. cayenne pepper
4 cloves garlic
4 heads dill or 6 tbsp. dill
 seed

2½ cups water
2½ cups vinegar
¼ cup salt
4 sterilized pint jars

Wash beans and remove stems. To each jar add: ¼ tsp. cayenne pepper, 1 clove garlic, 1 head dill or 1½ tbsp. dill seed, and then beans.

In large kettle, bring water, vinegar and salt to a boil. Pour mixture over beans, leaving ¼ inch of space at the top of each jar. Seal and process 15 minutes in boiling-water bath.

For boiling water bath, use large container with cover and dividing rack, deep enough to allow about 4 inches of space above jars. Fill container with enough water to cover jars 2 inches above tops. Heat water until almost boiling point, place jars into rack, cover, and when water reaches a boil, start the timing process according to recipe. Make sure jars are covered with water throughout processing. When processing time is reached, remove container from heat, allow water to cool completely, then remove jars. Makes four pints.

WATERMELON PICKLES

4 lbs. watermelon rind
½ oz. alum
½ gal. water
2 lbs. light brown sugar

1 pt. vinegar
2 tbsp. whole cloves
1½ tbsp. whole allspice
1 tbsp. whole ginger

Pare rind and cut into thick strips. Add alum to water; bring to boil and pour over rind. Let stand for about 1½ hours.

Drain; chill rind in cold water. Bring to boil sugar, vinegar, and spices (tied in cheesecloth bag). Add rind and cook 40 minutes. Place in 5 sterilized pint jars and seal. Makes five pints.

"PIC-NOSH" POTATO SALAD

6 hot boiled potatoes,
  peeled and sliced
3 strips cooked crisp Beef
  Frye, crumbled
¼ cup finely chopped green
  onion tops
¼ cup finely chopped onion

¼ cup finely chopped celery
¼ cup finely chopped
  parsley
4 hard-cooked eggs
2 tsp. salt
¼ tsp. pepper
⅔ cup mayonnaise

Toss all ingredients in large bowl. Add mayonnaise and mix well. Chill and serve. Serves eight.

POOR BOY SANDWICH #1

1 loaf French bread
6 or 7 slices roast beef
6 slices creole tomato
3 slices onion
shredded lettuce

mayonnaise
kosher dill slices
dash Tabasco sauce
gravy

Warm bread in oven. While still warm, spread with mayonnaise and roast beef. Add dash of Tabasco to hot gravy and pour over top. Close Arrange lettuce, tomatoes, pickles, and corned beef on bread. Close sandwich and serve.

POOR BOY SANDWICH #2

1 French bread
6 to 7 slices hot corned beef
creole mustard
mayonnaise

slices of kosher dill pickle
6 or 7 slices creole tomato
shredded lettuce

Spread bread with mayonnaise on one side and mustard on other. Arrange lettuce, tomatoes, pickles,and corned beef on bread. Close sandwich and serve.

CAJUN KEBOBS

4 red apples, unpeeled
4 Polish kosher sausages

1 tbsp. cider or wine vinegar
caraway seeds

Alternate chunks of apple with cubes of sausage on skewers. Sprinkle lightly with vinegar and caraway seeds. Broil briefly, only until apple is tender, but not soft; turn to cook evenly. Serves four.

PLANTATION CHICKEN

2 frying chickens, cut up
Creole Bar-B-Q Sauce (see
recipe)

Soak chicken pieces in Bar-B-Q sauce 1 hour, turning occasionally. Remove chicken, reserving dressing. Place chicken on barbecue grill and brown on all sides.

Just before chicken is completely done, begin to baste with Bar-B-Q Sauce. Continue basting frequently until all sauce is used and chicken is done. Serves eight.

CREOLE BAR-B-Q SAUCE

1 pkg. onion soup mix
2 tbsp. brown sugar
⅛ tsp. cayenne pepper
¼ tsp. pepper
¼ cup tarragon vinegar
1 cup tomato juice

2 tsp. paprika
¼ tsp. chili powder
1 tsp. dry mustard
1 cup boiling water
¼ cup catsup

Combine all ingredients except catsup. Simmer 15 minutes or until thickened. Stir in catsup. Makes about 2 cups.

SHORT RIBS WITH
NOSHER'S BAR-B-Q SAUCE

3 lbs. short ribs
1 tsp. salt
⅛ tsp. pepper

2 large onions, chopped fine
1 lemon, thinly sliced

Cut meat into serving-size pieces. Spread meaty side up in shallow roasting pan. Sprinkle with salt and pepper and place 1 thin slice lemon on each piece. Sprinkle with chopped onion. Place uncovered in a 450-degree oven for 45 minutes.

Pour off grease and add Nosher's Bar-B-Q Sauce (see recipe). Leave pan uncovered and reduce heat to 350°; continue roasting for additional 1½ hours. Baste meat frequently, turning occasionally. Serves four to six.

NOSHER'S BAR-B-Q SAUCE

¾ cup tomato catsup
2 tbsp. vinegar
2 tbsp. Worcestershire
  sauce
1 tbsp. salt
¾ cup water

1 tsp. paprika
½ tsp. pepper
1 tsp. chili powder
dash cayenne pepper or
  Tabasco sauce

Combine all ingredients. Use to baste meat while broiling or for braising. Makes about one and three-quarters cups.

COUNTRY SIDE BAR-B-Q'D HOT DOGS

1 lb. kosher franks
¼ cup Bar-B-Q Sauce (see
  recipe)

Brown franks over grill; place in sauce and simmer an additional 20 to 30 minutes. Serve with sauce on toasted buns.

COUNTRY SIDE BAR-B-Q SAUCE

1 small onion, chopped
½ small green pepper,
  chopped
2 tbsp. vegetable oil

1 tsp. mustard
1 tsp. chili powder
½ tsp. salt
1 tbsp. vinegar

Cook onion and green pepper in vegetable oil in heavy iron skillet for five minutes on slow fire. Add remaining ingredients. Serves eight.

GLAZED PICNIC "SHAM"

4 lbs. corned-beef brisket,
  boiled and cooled
1 cup packed dark brown
  sugar
1 tbsp. cornstarch
1 tsp. dry mustard

whole cloves
1 20-oz. can pineapple
  slices
liquid from pineapple
maraschino cherries

Place cooked corned beef in shallow baking dish with flat side up. Score fat. Stud with cloves.

Mix together sugar, mustard, and pineapple juice to form a paste; pour over meat. Decorate with pineapple slices and cherries, securing with toothpicks.

Preheat oven to 300°. Bake 30 to 40 minutes or until paste is glazed and meat is hot. Serves eight to ten.

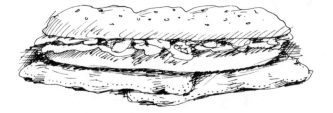

COTTON-PICKIN' EGGS

6 hard-cooked eggs
1 rib celery
salt and pepper
Tabasco sauce (optional)

8 pimento-stuffed olives
mayonnaise
parsley

Slice eggs in half lengthwise. Remove yolk and place in wooden bowl; add olives and celery and chop fine.

Add enough mayonnaise to soften mixture. Salt and pepper to taste. For extra tang, add dash of Tabasco sauce. Stuff into egg whites and garnish with sprig of parsley. Makes twelve.

CALAS MUFFINS

1 cup cooked rice
¾ cup nondairy creamer
¼ cup water
2 eggs, beaten
5 tbs. vegetable cooking oil

1½ cups sifted flour
2 tsp. sugar
½ tsp. salt
3 tsp. baking powder

Beat rice, nondairy creamer mixed with water, eggs, and oil together. Sift dry ingredients and add to mixture, mixing only enough to combine.

Fill well-greased muffin pans ⅔ full and bake in 400-degree oven for 25 minutes. Makes twelve muffins.

DEEP DELTA PEACH PIE

¾ cup sugar
¼ tsp. cinnamon
2 to 3 tbsp. flour
2 tbsp. pareve margarine

5 cups sliced, peeled fresh
   peaches
1 recipe pie pastry

Combine sugar, flour, and cinnamon. Add to peaches; mix slightly. Divide pastry in half. Roll half of dough to fit bottom of 9-inch pie pan. Spoon peaches into pie and dot with margarine. Roll remaining pastry into square about 10 inches by 10 inches. Cut pastry into 12 strips about ¾ inch wide. Make lattice top crust by placing six strips across pie and six strips down. Flute edges. Prick with fork at intervals along strips and edges. Bake at 400° for 45 to 50 minutes.

BANDANA BREAD

½ cup pareve margarine
2 eggs
1 tsp. baking soda
1 cup mashed bananas
1 cup sugar

2 cups flour
½ tsp. cinnamon
½ tsp. salt
½ cup chopped pecans

Cream margarine and sugar thoroughly. Add eggs, beating until blended. Sift together dry ingredients and add to mixture. Blend in bananas and nuts.

Pour mixture into a greased 9- by 5-inch loaf pan and bake in a 350-degree oven for 1 hour. Cool slightly before removing from pan.

GALLERY GLAZED STRAWBERRY PIE

1½ qts. fresh strawberries
2½ tbsp. cornstarch
few drops red food coloring
½ cup cold water

1 cup sugar
1 tbsp. pareve margarine
1 9-inch pastry shell, baked

Wash and hull strawberries. Place 1 quart of the berries in the pastry shell.

Crush remaining ½ quart of berries and combine with water, sugar, and cornstarch in a saucepan. Boil 2 minutes or until clear. Add margarine and sufficient red food coloring to give it an attractive color. Strain. Spoon glaze over the strawberry-filled pastry shell and cool.

July

July

Soul Food on the Levee

Louisiana is one of the lowest and most level states in the Union. Add to this the geographic location of the mighty Mississippi River and you have a state where over one-third of its area would be flooded each time the water level in the river became dangerously high if protective measures were not taken.

Early French and Spanish settlers were aware that the overflow of swollen waters caused widespread devastation. To prevent such catastrophes, they constructed walls along the banks of the river that were wide enough on the top to be used as roads. These levees, from the French word *lever* meaning "to raise," were their means of protection.

The first Mississippi River levee was built in New Orleans in 1719 and was only three feet in height. Today these embankments are often fifteen to thirty feet high. More than 2,500 miles of levees now line the banks of the river.

Levees are used extensively for purposes other than that for which they were designed: a bridle path for equestrians, an unbroken stretch of land for biking, an exercise and training ground for pets, a place to meditate, a good location to catch a riverbend view of the skyline . . . and a site for still another ethnic tradition.

New Orleans, you see, is a most cosmopolitan city. Although the French and Spanish were the founding fathers, immigrants from throughout the world came South and remained. The Germans, for one, comprised a sizeable settlement. They made the Deltaland home, lending even more customs to the potpourri of New Orleans culture.

On Thanksgiving Day, Germans, laden with pieces of wood, wend their way to the levee. Here they begin to pile their logs in mounds or in such shapes as log cabins and tepees. Each day they return, continuing the ritual until Christmas Eve. On that night, bonfires are lit and the wooden structures are set ablaze. According to legend, these fires light the way for St. Nick and guide him to those who have settled so far from their ancestral homeland.

Levees are an integral part of the city in much the same way "soul" is to our food. Although created by the American blacks, soul food belongs to the South. Ingenious black cooks created this simple yet enormously satisfying home-cooked food from the barest essentials, and served it with loving care. Soul food was added to New Orleans' unique cuisine and like the levee became a vital and essential part of the city.

July

Soul Food Potpourri

Appetizers:

Mother's Meatballs
Fish-Pole Fingers
Tartar Sauce
Giblet Jambalaya

Salads:

Delta Potato Salad
Auntée Chicken Salad
Big Mama's Macaroni Salad

Entrées:

Creole-Style Red Beans and Rice
Back-a-Town Red Beans
Cuzzin Caldonia's Chicken-Fried Steak
White Beans and Sham Hocks
Tabernacle Turkey Jambalaya
"Where Y'at" Fricassee
Dumplings from Downtown
Bonnie's Stewed Chicken
North Claiborne Stuffed Green Peppers
South Claiborne Stuffed Green Peppers
Pot Poulet

Vegetables:

Soulful Turnip Greens
French Market Field Peas
Sunday's Squash Fritters
Cajun Coush Coush

Desserts:

Gospel Yam Pie
Brother's Blackberry Pie
Pastor's Plantains
Beulah's Sweet Potato Pudding

MOTHER'S MEATBALLS

1 lb. ground beef
½ lb. ground veal
1 cup bread crumbs
½ cup chili sauce
1 egg
¼ cup minced onion

2 tbsp. minced parsley
1½ tsp. salt
½ tsp. Tabasco sauce
½ tsp. garlic powder
3 tbsp. pareve margarine

Combine beef, veal, bread crumbs, chili sauce, egg, onion, parsley, salt, Tabasco, and garlic powder. Shape mixture into 1-inch balls. Fry in small amount of margarine a few at a time, adding additional margarine as needed.

Spear each meatball with toothpick. Keep warm in chafing dish. Makes about eight dozen.

FISH-POLE FINGERS

2 tenderloins trout, cut up
   into finger-size pieces
2 eggs, beaten
1 cup flour
½ tsp. Seasonall

1 tbsp. Worcestershire
   sauce
1 tsp. Tabasco sauce
1 cup cornmeal
oil for frying

Pat each piece of fish dry. Add Seasonall to flour and mix well. Dip fish pieces in flour one at a time. Stir Worcestershire sauce and Tabasco sauce into beaten egg. Dip floured fish pieces into egg mixture and then into cornmeal.

Heat oil in heavy skillet. Fry a few pieces at a time, cooking until pieces begin to float on the surface of the oil. Turn over and finish cooking (about 10 minutes). Drain on paper towels and serve with Tartar Sauce (see recipe). Makes about twelve "fingers."

TARTAR SAUCE

1 cup mayonnaise
10 pimento-stuffed olives,
  chopped fine
2 ribs celery, chopped fine

juice from ½ lemon
1 clove garlic, chopped fine
salt and pepper to taste

Cut mayonnaise with lemon juice and mix well. Add olives, celery, garlic, salt, and pepper to taste. Mix well and refrigerate. This is a fine accompaniment to fish dishes. Makes one cup.

GIBLET JAMBALAYA

1 lb. chicken livers,
  broiled and cut in half
1 lb. gizzards
3 tbsp. pareve margarine
1¼ cups long-grain rice
1 tbsp. salt
1 clove garlic, minced
¾ cup diced onions

¾ cup chopped celery
5 large creole tomatoes,
  diced
1 bay leaf, crumbled
½ tsp. thyme
1 10½-oz. can chicken
  consommé, undiluted

Slice gizzards into thin pieces. Heat margarine in large heavy skillet and sauté gizzard slices a few minutes until slightly cooked. Stir in rice, salt, garlic, and onions. Add celery, tomatoes, bay leaf, thyme, and consommé. Lower heat and stir mixture just enough to thoroughly mix ingredients. Remove from heat and mix in livers. Place in 2-quart casserole dish, cover, and bake in 350-degree oven for 1 hour. Stir once more to distribute ingredients. Cover again and continue cooking an additional few minutes if necessary, or until liquids are absorbed. Serves six.

DELTA POTATO SALAD

2 large potatoes, cooked
  and diced
2 ribs celery
1 tbsp. tarragon vinegar
1 tsp. chopped chives
1 tsp. prepared mustard
1 tbsp. sweet pickle relish

4 hard-cooked eggs
½ cup mayonnaise
½ tsp. onion powder
½ tsp. parsley flakes
¼ tsp. Accent
salt and pepper to taste

Boil potatoes in jackets until easily pierced with a fork. Store in refrigerator overnight.

Peel potatoes and dice into ½-inch cubes; dice cooked eggs; chop celery into coarse pieces. Toss all three together.

Cut mayonnaise with tarragon vinegar and mustard, mixing until smooth and well blended. Add chives, onion powder, parsley flakes, relish, salt, pepper, and Accent; blend well. Pour mayonnaise mixture over potatoes, eggs, and celery. Mix well. Refrigerate until ready to serve. Serves four.

AUNTÉE CHICKEN SALAD

1 cup mayonnaise
½ tsp. Tabasco sauce
½ tsp. salt
2 tbsp. vinegar
2 tsp. grated onion
3 cups cooked diced
  chicken

1 cup diced celery
2 hard-cooked eggs,
  chopped
1 tbsp. chopped green
  pepper (optional)

Blend mayonnaise with Tabasco sauce, salt, vinegar, onion, and green pepper (if desired). Toss diced chicken, celery, and chopped eggs in large bowl. Add dressing and toss lightly. Refrigerate 2 to 3 hours before serving. Serves four.

BIG MAMA'S MACARONI SALAD

2 cups cooked elbow
  macaroni
1 cup mayonnaise
2 tbsp. tarragon vinegar
2 tbsp. creole mustard
¼ cup diced sweet pickles
1 tsp. salt
2 tbsp. minced onions

2 tbsp. chopped pimento
2 cups cold cuts (corned
  beef, pastrami, or
  salami), cut in bite-size
  pieces
1 tbsp. green pepper
  (optional)

Cook and drain macaroni. Place in large bowl and chill.

Mix together mayonnaise, vinegar, mustard, salt, sweet pickles, onions, pimento, and green pepper (if desired). Add to macaroni and toss. Add cold cuts to macaroni mixture and gently toss once more. Refrigerate until ready to serve. Serves six to eight.

CREOLE-STYLE RED BEANS AND RICE

1 lb. red beans
8 cloves garlic, chopped
1 rib celery, chopped
¼ lb. salami
1 lb. smoked sausage
1 large onion, chopped

¼ green pepper, chopped
1 tsp. sugar
salt and pepper to taste
pinch thyme
1 lb. weiners

Wash beans thoroughly; cover with water and place on medium fire.

Chop sausage and salami and add to beans; add garlic, celery, onions, green pepper, sugar, and thyme. Continue cooking until beans are soft, adding more water if necessary.

When beans are soft, add weiners, sliced in 1-inch pieces, and salt and pepper to taste. Cook until gravy is thick and creamy. Serve over steamed rice. Serves eight to ten.

BACK-A-TOWN RED BEANS

2 lbs. red beans, washed
3 large onions, chopped
1 green pepper, chopped
1 tbsp. parsley flakes
3 cloves garlic, minced
1 tsp. oregano
1 lb. kosher hot sausages
½ cup catsup
dash Tabasco sauce

½ lb. Beef Frye
5 ribs celery, chopped
1 bunch shallots, chopped
2 bay leaves
1 lb. beef short ribs
1 8-oz. can tomato sauce
2 tbsp. Worcestershire
     sauce
salt and pepper

Fry Beef Frye, drain on paper towels, and crumble into pieces. Reserve drippings. Place beans in large pot with short ribs, sliced sausages, and Beef Frye. Cover with water and cook on medium fire. Sauté shallots, onions, and garlic in a frying pan until light brown in Beef-Frye drippings. Add green pepper and celery and continue frying until celery is limp. Add parsley and catsup and cook for 5 minutes. Stir in bay leaf, Worcestershire sauce, salt, pepper, Tabasco, and oregano. Add this mixture to red beans and cook 3 hours or more, stirring occasionally, until beans are tender. Add small amount of water during last ½ hour of cooking, if necessary, to prevent beans from sticking to bottom of pan. Serve with long-grain white rice. (This recipe freezes well.) Serves twelve to fifteen.

CUZZIN CALDONIA'S CHICKEN-FRIED STEAK

6 thin slices veal (about 3
   by 4 inches)
oil for frying
1 egg, beaten

salt and pepper
½ cup pareve seasoned
   bread crumbs

Rinse veal cutlets and dry well. Season with salt and pepper. Dip each cutlet in beaten egg and roll in bread crumbs. Fry until golden brown on both sides in hot fat. Serves three.

WHITE BEANS AND SHAM HOCKS

2 cups white beans
1 large onion, chopped
2 carrots, diced
2 cloves garlic, chopped
2 Italian hot sausages, cut
  in 1-inch slices
1 tsp. pepper
½ tsp. oregano

6 cups cold water
½ cup parsley
3 tbsp. sugar
5 pieces chuck, about 2
  inches thick
2 tbsp. Worcestershire
  sauce
salt to taste

Rinse white beans and pick out any bad ones. Combine all ingredients in a large covered pot, add water, and bring to boil. Reduce heat and simmer for 2½ to 3 hours or until beans are tender. Remove meat, cut and dice into smaller pieces, and return to beans. Serve with rice. Serves four.

TABERNACLE TURKEY JAMBALAYA

1 medium onion,
  chopped
2 cloves garlic, minced
1 green pepper, chopped
  fine
2 tbsp. vegetable shortening
1 tbsp. flour
2 cups canned whole
  tomatoes
pinch thyme

½ bay leaf, crushed
1 tsp. salt
1 tsp. cayenne pepper
4 cups boiling water
3 cups diced cooked turkey
1 cup rice
dash Tabasco sauce
1 tbsp. Worcestershire
  sauce

Sauté onion, garlic, and green pepper in vegetable shortening until transparent. Make roux by stirring in flour and continue stirring until smooth. Add tomatoes, thyme, bay leaf, salt, pepper, and water and simmer for 10 minutes. Add diced turkey. Bring to a boil and stir in rice, Tabasco, and Worcestershire. Cook additional 20 to 25 minutes, stirring occasionally. Serves six.

"WHERE Y'AT" FRICASSEE

1 4-lb. chicken, cut up
salt and pepper to taste
1 onion, chopped
1 tbsp. vegetable shortening
1 bay leaf
1 tbsp. Worcestershire
  sauce

1 sprig thyme
1 tbsp. flour
1 tbsp. minced parsley
3 cups boiling water

Season chicken with salt and pepper. Sauté onion in hot shortening. Add flour and chicken and brown lightly on all sides over low heat. Add seasonings and water. Bring to boil; cover, reduce heat, and simmer until tender (about 1 hour). Serves six.

DUMPLINGS FROM DOWNTOWN

1 cup flour
½ tsp. salt
⅓ cup water

2 tsp. baking powder
1 egg
2 cups clear chicken broth

Stir together flour, baking powder, and salt. Beat egg and water until well mixed; stir into flour mixture until well blended.

Bring broth to boil. Drop dumpling mixture by teaspoon in broth and boil uncovered for 2 minutes. Simmer covered until cooked through (about 20 minutes). Dumplings can be served with soup or in chicken fricassee. Two dumplings per portion. Serves four.

BONNIE'S STEWED CHICKEN

1 3-lb chicken, cut up
4 tbsp. vegetable oil
¾ cup green pepper, cut in
thin strips
1 8-oz. can tomato sauce
½ tsp. pepper
¼ tsp. thyme
½ cup flour

¾ cup sliced onion
2 cloves garlic, chopped fine
2½ cups canned whole
tomatoes
1 bay leaf
½ tsp. oregano
½ tsp. salt

Dip chicken pieces in flour. Heat oil in skillet, brown chicken, and remove from skillet. Add onion, green pepper, and garlic and sauté, adding more oil if necessary. Add chicken and remaining ingredients. Cover and cook over low heat, stirring occasionally, for 1½ hours or until chicken is tender. Serves four to five.

NORTH CLAIBORNE
STUFFED GREEN PEPPERS

6 bell peppers, cleaned
and cut in half
2½ lbs. ground beef
2 loaves French bread
6 eggs
¼ cup parsley, chopped fine

1 large onion, minced
1 rib celery, chopped fine
½ lb. pareve margarine
1 tsp. thyme
salt and pepper to taste

Melt margarine in large skillet. Add parsley, onion, and celery. Simmer on low flame about 20 minutes. Add ground beef and cook 20 minutes, stirring constantly.

Soak French bread in small amount of water in large pan. Squeeze out liquid, add eggs, and mix thoroughly. Add beef mixture and stir together. Add thyme, salt, and pepper. Stuff bell-pepper halves with mixture; top with bread crumbs and dot with margarine.

Place in large baking pan with about ½ inch of water in bottom. Bake in 350-degree oven for 45 minutes to 1 hour until brown. Serves twelve.

SOUTH CLAIBORNE
STUFFED GREEN PEPPERS

2 lbs. ground beef
1 green pepper, chopped
2 ribs celery, chopped
12 parboiled medium-size
  green peppers
salt, pepper, cayenne

2 onions, chopped
3 green onions, chopped
2 cloves garlic, minced
2 tbsp. cooking oil
2 eggs, beaten
2 cups cooked rice

Sauté onions and green pepper in a little oil until golden brown. Add celery, green onions, and garlic and sauté for 10 minutes. Add meat and brown; drain off excess grease.

Add salt, pepper, and eggs. Return to fire and cook until well blended. Remove from fire and toss rice with meat mixture.

Cut caps off green peppers and scoop out insides. Drain and stuff peppers with meat mixture. Sprinkle with bread crumbs and dot with pareve margarine. Bake in shallow pan containing enough water to cover bottom for 30 minutes at 325°. Serves twelve.

POT POULET

1 frying chicken
1 cup flour
1 tsp. salt
1 tsp. pepper

½ tsp. onion powder
¼ tsp. garlic powder
½ tsp. paprika
4 to 5 slices Beef Frye

Cut fryer into serving pieces. Place flour in paper bag, add seasonings, and shake well. Dip fryer pieces into seasoned flour.

Fry Beef Frye until crisp and remove from frying pan. Add fryer to Beef-Frye drippings and cook until brown; turn and brown other side.

Reduce heat and add small amount of hot water, stirring until smooth. Cover and cook until fryer is tender (about 30 to 40 minutes). Serves four.

SOULFUL TURNIP GREENS

½ lb. kosher salami or
  smoked sausage
1 onion, chopped
salt and pepper

2 bunches turnip greens,
  washed thoroughly and
  stemmed

Add salami or smoked sausage, onion, salt, and pepper to greens. (Add no water.) Cover and cook slowly until meat and greens are tender (about 20 minutes). Serves four.

Mustard greens or collard greens can be substituted for turnip greens.

FRENCH MARKET FIELD PEAS

1 pt. field peas
¼ lb. kosher smoked
  sausage

1 small onion, chopped
1 qt. cold water

Shell and remove any bad peas. Wash and drain. Sauté sausage and onion for 5 minutes. Add peas and water; cover and bring to a boil. Turn heat to simmer and cook peas until tender (about 30 minutes). Serves four.

SUNDAY'S SQUASH FRITTERS

2 cups grated summer
  squash
¼ tsp. grated onion
dash pepper
1 tsp. salt

6 tbsp. flour
2 eggs
2 tsp. melted pareve
  margarine
2 tsp. sugar (optional)

Combine squash, onions, pepper, sugar, salt, and flour. Beat eggs and add to squash mixture. Add margarine. Drop by the tablespoon into melted margarine in skillet. Cook on both sides until light brown. Serve immediately. Serves six.

CAJUN COUSH COUSH

2 cups cornmeal
½ tsp. salt
1½ cups boiling water

2 tsp. baking powder
3 eggs, beaten
1 tsp. shortening

Stir cornmeal and salt into water. Cool and add baking powder and eggs. Preheat skillet containing shortening and pour in mixture. Cook over medium heat for 5 minutes. Scrape bottom and sides of skillet and cook 10 minutes longer. Serves eight.

GOSPEL YAM PIE

4 fresh yams, baked, or 2
   cups canned yams
1 unbaked pie crust
1 cup nondairy creamer
½ cup water
1 cup brown sugar

1 tbsp. pareve margarine
3 eggs, beaten
1 tsp. cinnamon
1 tsp. nutmeg
1 tsp. salt
½ cup chopped pecans

Mash yams well. Stir in hot nondairy creamer mixed with water, sugar, margarine, cinnamon, nutmeg, and salt. Gradually mix in beaten eggs. Pour into unbaked pie shell and sprinkle top with chopped pecans. Bake in 425° oven until set (about 35 to 40 minutes).

BROTHER'S BLACKBERRY PIE

3 cups blackberries
2 tbsp. lemon juice
1 recipe pastry for two-crust
  pie

1 cup sugar
⅛ tsp. salt
1 tbsp. butter (or pareve
  margarine)

Combine berries, sugar, flour, lemon juice, and salt. Line a pie pan with pastry and add filling. Dot with butter and cover with top crust. Make a few 1-inch slits in top crust.

Bake in 450-degree oven for 10 minutes. Reduce heat to 350° and continue baking 25 to 30 minutes longer.

PASTOR'S PLANTAINS

3 plantains
1 cup brown sugar

1 cup hot water
vegetable shortening

Slice plantains lengthwise about ¼ inch thick. Fry in as little fat as possible; drain. Heat sugar and water in a saucepan, stirring until sugar is melted. Put plantains in syrup and cook gently 15 minutes. Serves four to six.

BEULAH'S SWEET POTATO PUDDING

1 cup sugar
1 cup brown sugar
1½ cups nondairy creamer
½ cup water
3 cups grated sweet
  potatoes
4 eggs, beaten

¼ stick melted pareve
  margarine
½ cup seedless raisins
1½ cups chopped pecans
1 cup shredded coconut
½ cup drained crushed
  pineapple

Combine all ingredients in bowl and blend thoroughly. Pour into casserole dish. Bake at 350° for 1 hour or until set. Serves ten.

August

August

Steamboat Seafood Secrets

When Hernando de Soto discovered the Mississippi River in 1541, there was already activity up and down the river. Indians paddled their canoes upstream, eager to trade. Later French and Spanish explorers took to the waters in *pirogues* (hollowed-out cypress logs), and in the days when cotton was king, flatboats and keelboats plied the river laden with cargo. The Mississippi River, then as now, was the lifeline of commerce and industry in the region.

Then came the steamboat. The *New Orleans* was the first such vessel to navigate the western waters. Built by Nicholas J. Roosevelt, it left Pittsburgh in December 1811 and in January 1812 docked in the city of New Orleans, for which it was named. The golden age of the paddlewheeler had begun, opening a new era in transportation and commerce. Now it was possible to carry goods and passengers upstream as well as downstream; everything once confined to New Orleans could be shipped to cities outside the Delta region.

With the arrival of cargo-laden and luxurious passenger ships, the docks came alive with colorful characters: banana peddlers, women selling homemade pralines, others with baskets atop their heads shouting "berries, berries, fresh berries for sale." Musicians, seated on bales of cotton, livened the scene with their haunting melodies, and fishermen sold their catches.

Today modern diesels, barges, ferries, passenger liners, tugboats, and naval craft from the four corners of the earth can be seen in the world's third largest port. They come not only for commerce and trade, but to take advantage of the Mississippi's bounty of the sea. Ship captains delight their passengers with a dinner on board, featuring fresh seafood specialties. Freezers are stocked with fresh catch to bring home, for nowhere else is seafood as plentiful, as varied, and as delicious as that which comes from the Mississippi and her tributaries.

So in appreciation of Old Man River and the steamboats that first carried our seafoods outside the city, we have divulged our secrets—the secrets for creating Creole jambalayas without shrimp and gumbos without pork or crabs, yet retaining the succulent Creole seasonings and spicy Kosher flavors. In other words, the secrets of an innovative new culinary form: Kosher Creole cooking, New Orleans style!

August

I.

Oysters Mock-a-feller
River Filé Gumbo
Sailor's Salad
Cargo Casserole
Riverfront Tomatoes
Loxiana Eggplant
Pelican's Nest

II.

"Oy!-Sters" Off the Half Shell
Faux Pas "Turtle" Soup
Water Crescent Salad
Secret Seafood Stuffed Trout
Seafood Dressing
Steamboat Squash
Tugboat Turnips with Hollandaise Sauce
Banana Barge Ambrosia

III.

Snapper Cocktail with Sauce Louie
Baleboosteh's Bouillabaisse
River Basin Salad
Toll Bridge Dressing
Sea Dogs' Tipsy Trout
Capt'in Andy's Wax Beans
Down the River Rice
Cabin Boy's Cushaw
Foghorn Fig Cake

OYSTERS MOCK-A-FELLER

18 gefilte fish pieces in jar
⅓ bunch spinach
6 shallots
3 ribs celery
⅓ bunch parsley
⅓ head lettuce
1 stick pareve margarine
(softened at room
temperature)

1 tbsp. Worcestershire
sauce
1 tsp. anchovy paste
dash Tabasco sauce
¾ ounce 80-proof absinthe
⅓ tsp. salt
½ cup seasoned bread
crumbs

Chop all greens fine and mix with margarine and half of bread crumbs. Reserve remaining bread crumbs. Add remaining ingredients, except fish pieces, and blend thoroughly.

Drain gefilte fish, slice in half, and place in oven-proof, shell-shaped ramekins. Set shells in a pan of hot, coarse kosher rock salt. Spread sauce over fish pieces and sprinkle with remaining bread crumbs.

Bake at 450° about 25 minutes; then place under broiler to brown. Serves six.

RIVER FILÉ GUMBO

1 10-oz. pkg. frozen sliced
  okra
⅓ cup Beef-Frye drippings
  or vegetable shortening
1 cup shallots with tops,
  chopped
1 cup diced green celery
1 clove garlic, minced
¼ cup flour
2 cups hot water

1 16-oz. can stewed
  tomatoes
salt to taste
¼ tsp. pepper
1 bay leaf
few drops Tabasco sauce
1 15½-oz. can salmon
dash filé
1⅓ cups cooked rice

Thaw okra and sauté in Beef-Frye drippings or vegetable shortening for 10 minutes, stirring occasionally. Add onions, celery, and garlic and cook about 5 more minutes. Stir in flour. Add hot water, stirring constantly, and cook until slightly thickened. Add tomatoes, salt, pepper, and bay leaf and cover. Simmer for additional 20 minutes on low flame. Remove bay leaf and add Tabasco sauce.

Debone and skin salmon and add to gumbo. Heat thoroughly. Add dash of filé just before serving. Serve in soup bowls over hot rice. Serves four.

SAILOR'S SALAD

2 3¼-oz. cans boneless
  sardines
1½ cups diced celery
¼ cup diced kosher dill
  pickle

1 tsp. vinegar
¼ cup mayonnaise
1 tbsp. creole mustard
lettuce leaves

Drain sardines and combine with celery and pickle. Sprinkle vinegar over mixture and let marinate about 10 minutes.

Add mustard to mayonnaise and blend well; add other ingredients. Chill and serve on lettuce leaves. Serves five.

CARGO CASSEROLE

1 2-oz. jar kosher roe
3 anchovy fillets
3 eggs, well beaten
1 cup nondairy creamer
¼ cup water
1 tsp. Worcestershire sauce

dash Tabasco sauce
pinch thyme
salt and pepper to taste
chopped chives and sliced
  creole tomatoes for
  garnish

Mix roe and anchovy fillets well. Add eggs, nondairy creamer, water, Worcestershire sauce, Tabasco, thyme, salt, and pepper, and blend well. Pour into a greased 1-quart casserole. Bake in 400-degree oven about 35 minutes or until firm. Garnish with chopped chives and creole tomato slices. Serves four.

RIVERFRONT TOMATOES

1 27-oz. can spinach
1 large onion, chopped fine
⅛ tsp. pepper
1 tsp. salt
¼ tsp. oregano

3 tbsp. vegetable shortening
2 eggs, beaten
6 large ripe tomatoes
bread crumbs
pareve margarine

Drain and rinse spinach. Pick stems from leaves and squeeze dry. Sauté onion in shortening until transparent; add salt, pepper, and oregano, and stir. Mix spinach and eggs together. Add to onions and cook until moderately dry, stirring often so mixture does not stick to bottom of pan.

Cut tops off tomatoes. Scoop out pulp (save for making gravies, jambalayas, etc.). Stuff tomatoes with spinach mixture. Sprinkle with bread crumbs and dot with margarine. Place tomatoes in baking pan and bake at 350° for 30 minutes. Serves six.

LOXIANA EGGPLANT

1 large eggplant
2 onions, chopped
1 clove garlic, chopped
½ tsp. pepper
½ tsp. oregano
2 tbsp. Worcestershire
  sauce
4 slices bread
6 slices Beef Frye

2 ribs celery, finely chopped
1 tsp. chopped chives
dash Tabasco sauce
½ tsp. parsley flakes
2 slices lox, cut in ½- by
  ½-inch pieces
1 egg, beaten
bread crumbs
pareve margarine

Slice eggplant in half lengthwise. Place in pot and pour in enough cold salted water to cover eggplant. Heat to boiling. Lower heat, cover, and continue cooking until tender (about 25 to 30 minutes). Remove and allow to cool.

Scrape out eggplant, carefully preserving shell, and drain in colander. Fry Beef Frye until crisp. Remove and reserve drippings. When cool, crumble into small pieces.

Soak bread in small amount of water; squeeze out excess liquid and set aside. Sauté onions, celery, garlic, pepper, oregano, Worcestershire, chives, Tabasco, and parsley in Beef Frye drippings, adding a few tablespoons of cooking oil to drippings if needed. Remove with slotted spoon and place in large bowl. Add Beef Frye, eggplant, egg, and bread. Mix well; return to pan, and continue to cook a few minutes, stirring constantly so mixture does not stick to bottom of pan. Remove from heat and add pieces of lox; mix until lox is evenly distributed.

Stuff eggplant shells and sprinkle bread crumbs on top. Dot with margarine and place in shallow roasting pan. Bake in 350-degree oven for 30 minutes or until brown on top. Serves four.

PELICAN'S NEST

2 oz. semisweet
chocolate
1 qt. pareve lime ice sherbet

½ lb. moist shredded
coconut

Melt chocolate in top of double boiler. Place coconut in bowl and pour chocolate gradually over coconut, tossing lightly until evenly coated. Shape into 12 "nests" and place on baking sheets covered with aluminum foil. Place in refrigerator until hardened. Before serving place scoop of lime ice in each "nest." Serves twelve.

"OY!-STERS" OFF THE HALF SHELL

Serve two each of the following "Oy!-sters" on appetizer plate per person.

Veal "Oy!-sters"

2 lbs. veal
1 egg
salt and pepper

1 cup bread crumbs or
cornmeal

Cut veal in pieces the size of an oyster, dip in beaten egg, roll in bread crumbs or cornmeal, and season with salt and pepper. Fry in deep fat at 375 degrees until light brown. Serves six.

Corn "Oy!-sters"

2 cups corn pulp
2 eggs
2 tbsp. flour

2 tbsp. melted schmaltz
salt and pepper

Grate fresh corn from the cob with a coarse grater. Beat egg yolks and whites separately and add to grated corn along with flour, fat, salt, and pepper. Drop batter from a spoon into hot fat at 360 to 375 degrees and fry until light brown (2 to 3 minutes). Drain on soft paper. Serves six.

Cauliflower "Oy!-sters"

1 head cauliflower
2 eggs
2 tbsp. flour

2 tbsp. vegetable oil
salt and pepper

Place cauliflower in boiling water and parboil for 1 minute. Drain and cool. Cut into bite-size pieces. Beat eggs well; add flour, vegetable oil, salt, and pepper and mix until smooth. Dip cauliflower pieces into batter. Drop into hot oil and fry until light brown. Remove and drain on paper towels. Serves six.

FAUX PAS "TURTLE" SOUP

1 2-lb. red snapper
1 rib celery, chopped
2 shallots, chopped
1 white onion, minced
2 sprigs parsley
2 cloves garlic, minced
2 whole cloves garlic
1½ sticks pareve margarine
3 tbsp. flour

1 8-oz. can stewed
   tomatoes, drained
salt and pepper
1 tbsp. Worcestershire
   sauce
8 tbsp. sherry
1 large lemon, cut into 8
   slices
2 hard-cooked eggs, grated

Place whole fish in enough salted water to cover it and boil until tender. Remove and set aside to cool. When cool, dehead, debone, and cut into bite-size pieces. Continue to cook broth, skimming when necessary, until clear. Turn off fire and add celery, shallots, parsley, and garlic.

Make roux with flour and margarine in separate pan. Add minced white onion, tomato, minced garlic, Worcestershire sauce, salt, and pepper to taste. Simmer about 10 minutes.

Add roux to broth and cook about 1 hour. Strain soup. Add fish pieces and cook only until fish is heated through (about 1 minute). Add sherry and lemon slices before serving. Sprinkle grated egg on top of each bowl of soup. Serves eight.

WATER CRESCENT SALAD

1 bunch crisp watercress
1 hard-cooked egg, chopped
1 tsp. chopped onion
1 tsp. chopped celery

2 slices crisp Beef Frye,
   crumbled
½ cup French Dressing (see
   recipe)

Rinse watercress in cold water, wipe dry, and pull sprigs apart, discarding heavy stems. Add egg, onion, celery, and Beef Frye. Add French dressing and toss until evenly distributed. Serves five.

SECRET SEAFOOD STUFFED TROUT

4 fillets of trout (with skin
   left on)
bread crumbs
juice of 1 lemon

½ stick pareve margarine
Seafood Dressing (see
   recipe)

SEAFOOD DRESSING

2 shallots, chopped fine
2 medium white onions,
   minced
½ stick pareve margarine
½ tsp. salt
⅛ tsp. pepper
¼ tsp. garlic powder
1 tbsp. minced parsley

½ tsp. oregano
1 tbsp. Worcestershire
   sauce
6 slices white bread
1 large piece smoked trout
   (enough to yield ½ cup
   flaked meat)

Melt margarine in large heavy skillet. Sauté shallots and white onions until transparent. Remove from pan. Soak bread in water and squeeze out excess liquid. Add salt, pepper, garlic powder, parsley, oregano, Worcestershire sauce, and sautéed onions to bread. Mix well.

Return mixture to pan and cook on medium flame about 5 minutes, stirring constantly to avoid sticking. Remove mixture from pan and place in large bowl. Remove skin and bones from smoked trout. Flake meat into pieces about ½ inch thick. Fold gently into bread mixture.

Place trout fillets skin side down. With very sharp knife, make 3-inch slit down center of each fillet being careful not to cut through skin. Push meat to side, forming cavity for dressing. Place enough dressing into cavity to form large mound (about 2 tablespoons). Melt margarine in large, flat roasting pan; mix with lemon juice. Sprinkle bottom of pan with bread crumbs. Place stuffed, raw trout in pan, skin side down.

Bake in 425-degree oven for 40 to 45 minutes, basting occasionally with drippings. Skin side of fish will come out crisp and brown. Serves four.

STEAMBOAT SQUASH

3 medium-size acorn
  squash
6 tbsp. brown sugar
½ tsp. cinnamon

3 tbsp. melted pareve
  margarine
salt

Cut acorn squash in half. Scrape out seeds and fibers and sprinkle with salt. Brush with melted margarine. Place flat side down on cookie sheet and bake in 400-degree oven until soft (about 40 minutes).

Turn flat side up and brush again with melted margarine. Prick pulp with fork and sprinkle liberally with brown sugar and cinnamon mixture. Bake about 15 minutes longer. Serves six.

TUGBOAT TURNIPS WITH HOLLANDAISE SAUCE

3 tbsp. pareve margarine
3 cups diced cooked turnips
½ cup fresh or canned
  whole-kernel corn
1 medium onion, chopped
1 medium apple, cored and
  sliced

1 tsp. salt
¼ tsp. nutmeg
¼ cup Hollandaise Sauce
  (see recipe)

Melt margarine. Add turnips, corn, onions, apple pieces, salt, and nutmeg. Simmer until apple and onions are soft (about 15 minutes). Pour Hollandaise Sauce over turnips and serve. Serves six.

BANANA BARGE AMBROSIA

3 grapefruit, peeled and
  sectioned
1 cup coarsely chopped
  pitted dates

4 oranges, peeled and
  sectioned
2 cups sliced bananas
¾ cup flaked coconut

Layer grapefruit and orange sections, banana slices, and dates in glasses, sprinkling each layer with coconut. Chill several hours. Serves eight.

SNAPPER COCKTAIL WITH SAUCE LOUIE

3 qts. water
1 large onion, quartered
1 lemon, quartered
1 bag crab boil

½ cup salt
cayenne pepper to taste
1 3-lb. redfish, red snapper,
   or trout

Bring water to boil. Add onion, lemon, crab boil, salt, and cayenne. Boil for 10 minutes.

Remove head from fish; clean and scale. Wrap whole fish in cheesecloth and tie with string. Place in boiling seasoned water; cover and simmer for 25 minutes or until fish is cooked.

Remove fish and place on flat surface. Remove cheesecloth and allow to cool. When cool, skin and debone fish. Flake fish meat. Serve cold, in cocktail glasses, topped with Sauce Louie (see recipe). Serves six.

SAUCE LOUIE

1 cup mayonnaise
¼ cup French dressing
¼ cup catsup
¼ tsp. pepper

1½ tsp. Worcestershire
   sauce
¼ tsp. salt

Mix ingredients and chill. Makes one and a half cups.

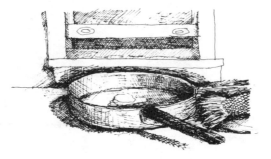

BALEBOOSTEH'S BOUILLABAISSE

1 bunch celery
3 medium white onions
2 bunches shallots
4 green peppers
3 cloves garlic
4 cups canned whole
  tomatoes
liquid from tomatoes

1 small bunch parsley
1 tsp. thyme
2 bay leaves
2 lbs. redfish
1 15½-oz. can pink salmon
½ cup white wine
2 tbsp. pareve margarine

Slice celery, shallots, green peppers, and garlic very thin. Sauté lightly in margarine. Cube tomatoes and add with liquid. Chop parsley fine and add together with thyme and bay leaves. Add 8 cups water and bring to a boil. Reduce heat and simmer about 1 hour.

Slice redfish into thin steaks. Place on cookie sheet and bake lightly (just long enough to seal in juices).

Add fish to vegetables and simmer on low heat for additional 30 minutes. Add salmon and continue to simmer another 5 minutes. Remove from heat and add wine. Serves eight.

RIVER BASIN SALAD

1 head lettuce
imitation bacon bits
4 hard-cooked eggs, chopped
2 shallots, chopped

1 avocado, chopped
Toll Bridge Dressing (see
  recipe)

Break up lettuce. Add imitation bacon bits, eggs, onion, and avocado. Toss lightly until evenly mixed and serve with Toll Bridge Dressing. Serves four.

TOLL BRIDGE DRESSING

1 2-oz. can anchovies
¼ tsp. garlic powder
2 shallots, chopped fine
2 tbsp. lime juice

4 tbsp. wine vinegar
1 tbsp. chopped parsley
1½ cups mayonnaise
1 tbsp. pepper

Place anchovies, garlic powder, shallots, lime juice, wine vinegar, and parsley in blender and mix well. Add mayonnaise and pepper and blend. Refrigerate overnight. Makes about one pint.

SEA DOGS' TIPSY TROUT

4 slices fillet trout
1 cup flour
1 tsp. pepper
½ tsp. onion powder
1 stick butter
⅓ cup dry cooking sherry
4 slices lemon
¾ cup milk

½ tsp. salt
½ tsp. oregano
½ tsp. parsley flakes
3 tbsp. Worcestershire
  sauce
juice from 1 lemon
⅓ cup water

Mix pepper, onion powder, salt, oregano, and parsley flakes with flour. Rinse and pat dry fillets. Dip in milk, then in seasoned flour. Melt butter in large skillet and brown fish on both sides over medium flame (turning only once). Remove from skillet, reserving drippings, and place in rectangular dish or baking pan.

Add Worcestershire sauce, lemon juice, and sherry to pan drippings. Slowly add water, stirring constantly about 2 minutes; pour over fish fillets. Place 1 slice lemon on each fillet. Cover and bake at 350° for 20 minutes and serve immediately. Serves four.

CAPT'IN ANDY'S WAX BEANS

2 tbsp. butter or pareve
   margarine
1 tsp. flour
1 medium onion, chopped
1 rib celery, chopped
1 carrot, grated

1 10½-oz. can tomatoes or 3
   medium-size ripe
   tomatoes, quartered
1 16-oz. can wax beans
salt and pepper to taste

Melt butter or margarine in large pan. Add flour and make roux. Add onion, celery, and carrot, stirring frequently. Cook over low flame about 5 minutes, continuing to stir, until vegetables are softened. Add tomatoes and cook rapidly on higher flamer for 10 minutes. Add beans, reduce heat, and simmer until sauce thickens slightly (about 10 minutes). Add salt and pepper and serve. Serves five.

DOWN THE RIVER RICE

½ tsp. salt
1⅓ cups orange juice
¼ cup chopped pecans

1⅓ cups Minute Rice
1½ tbsp. butter or pareve
   margarine

Bring orange juice to boil. Add salt and rice. Mix, cover, remove from heat. Let stand 5 minutes while rice absorbs orange flavor. Add butter or margarine and nuts; mix. Serves four.

CABIN BOY'S CUSHAW

1 medium-size cushaw
2 eggs
2 cups sugar
1 tbsp. honey

2 tsp. vanilla extract
2 sticks pareve margarine
pinch salt

Cut cushaw into pieces, removing seeds, and boil until tender. Peel and drain.

Heat 1½ sticks margarine and stir in sugar until mixture is brown. Add salt, honey, and cushaw and cook for 25 minutes. Remove from fire.

Beat eggs and stir into cushaw. Place in casserole dish and pour remaining melted margarine over top. Drizzle honey over top and bake additional 30 minutes in 325-degree oven. Serves six to eight.

FOGHORN FIG CAKE

½ cup shortening
1½ cups sugar
2 eggs, beaten
1 tsp. vanilla extract
1 cup brown sugar
2½ cups cake flour

½ tsp. salt
3 tsp. baking powder
1 cup milk
¼ cup butter
1 pt. fresh figs

Thoroughly cream shortening and sugar. Add eggs and vanilla extract; beat until fluffy. Add sifted dry ingredients alternately with milk, mixing thoroughly after each addition.

Sprinkle brown sugar into a skillet or deep layer-cake pan. Dot with butter. Arrange split figs to cover sugar; pour cake batter over figs. Bake at 350° for 40 to 60 minutes

When done, turn upside down on platter. Serve hot or cold with whipped cream.

Kosher Creole
Lagniappe

Bon Appétit and L'Chaim!

My how the time has flown! When someone (especially a cook) is busy, it's hard to believe that twelve festive months have passed. It's time for a break, maybe even a vacation. Perhaps the mini-descriptions of New Orleans' many attractions — the places to see, things to do, traditions of its people — have aroused your curiosity and interest. Maybe the brief insights into the unique culinary world of Kosher Creole cuisine have whetted your appetite, and you would like to see and taste it all for yourself.

Well, come on down and stay a while. As you can tell, there's always something cooking on the calendar and in the home for folks like you. In the summer, take a steamboat cruise; in the fall, the bayous beckon; in the winter, it's a sportsman's paradise; in spring, the magnolias are in bloom.

We invite you to browse around the Vieux Carré where it all began. See the mystery of voodooism; hear the plaintive cry of the jazzmen; march in a Mardi Gras parade; enjoy the potpourri that is so much a part of New Orleans. The Creole babies with flashing eyes are still selling their wares of exotic herbs, spices, and condiments in the French Quarter shops. Pick up an assortment to take back. The Kosher delicatessens are well stocked with Traditional products. Take some samplings of these, too.

Upon your return, try our recipes. They'll be a lasting reminder of New Orleans, the city famous for its cuisine: Creole, Kosher, and now — Kosher Creole.

As our cooking calendar and Hebrew lunar calendar come to a close, we wish you a new year of health, happiness, and many joyous occasions to entertain your family and friends.

Bon appétit and l'chaim!

Kosher Creole Lagniappe

Something Extra, Our Bonus to You:
Mock Sour Cream

September
Smoked Trout á la Creole
Chicken Genet

October
Creole Baked Fish
Acadian Trout Casserole

November
Faked Froglegs
Congo Square Tomatoes

December
Bandana Bananas
Creamy Pecan Pralines

January
Eggs Orleans
Eggs de Superdome

February
Strutters Spread
Doubloon Dip

March
Piano Roll Potatoes
Swinging Red Bean Soup

April
Passover Pain Perdu
Spring Fiesta Baked Flounder

May
Magnolia Blossom Pudding
Pecan Brittle

June
Pickled Green Peppers
River Road Corn Relish

July
Nonnie's Chocolate Icebox Pie
"Nu-Aw-Luns" Apple Pie

August
Poisson Sauce
Gang Plank Salad

MOCK SOUR CREAM

1 tbsp. pareve margarine
1 tbsp. cornstarch

1 cup nondairy creamer
1 tbsp. distilled vinegar

Melt margarine on low flame. Remove from fire and stir in cornstarch until smooth. Add about 2 tablespoons creamer and beat with spoon until smooth.

Return to low fire and add small amounts of creamer at a time, stirring constantly until creamer is gone.

Continue cooking and stirring until mixture comes to a boil. Lower flame and continue stirring until mixture is the consistency of custard.

Remove from fire, add vinegar, and mix well. Allow to cool. (Mixture will thicken more as it cools.) Makes one-half cup.

SMOKED TROUT À LA CREOLE

1 large onion, chopped
½ cup celery, chopped
2 tbsp. vegetable oil
2 creole tomatoes, minced
2 cups water
1 lb. smoked trout, skinned, deboned, and broken into pieces

1 medium bell pepper, chopped
1 bay leaf
salt and pepper to taste
3 cups cooked long-grain white rice
½ cup chopped shallots
¼ cup minced parsley

Sauté onion and celery in vegetable oil. Add minced tomatoes and continue cooking for about 5 minutes. Add water, smoked trout, bell pepper, and bay leaf. Bring to boil. Reduce heat and simmer for 1 hour.

Season with salt and pepper. Add rice, shallots, and parsley. Cover and remove from heat. Allow to stand about ½ hour before serving. Garnish with additional parsley sprigs, if desired. Serves four to six.

CHICKEN GENET

2 frying chickens, cut up
1 orange, sliced thin
1 lemon, sliced thin
2 large onions, sliced thin
1 chicken bouillon cube
1/4 cup hot water
1/4 cup honey

1/8 tsp. cloves
1/8 tsp. rosemary
1/8 tsp. garlic powder
1/4 tsp. salt
1/4 tsp. pepper
vegetable oil to cover
    bottom of skillet

Heat oil in skillet until hot (375 degrees). Brown chicken on all sides and remove to baking pan. Sauté onions until golden brown. Mix all seasonings together, sprinkle over chicken; place slices of lemon, oranges and sautéed onions over chicken.

Dissolve bouillon cube in water. Add honey and bouillon to chicken. Bake in 350-degree oven until chicken is tender and very brown (about 1 hour). Serves six.

CREOLE BAKED FISH

1 medium onion,
    chopped
2 tbsp. shortening
2 cups cooked or canned
    whole tomatoes
1 bay leaf
2 lbs. fish filets
1/4 cup chopped green
    pepper

2 tbsp. flour
1 tsp. salt
1/8 tsp. pepper
1 10-oz. pkg. frozen yellow
    corn or 1 1/2 cup cooked
    corn

Sauté onion and green pepper in shortening until tender. Add flour and blend. Then add tomatoes, salt, pepper, and bay leaf; bring to a boil. Cover and simmer 10 minutes. Add corn and cook over low heat 10 minutes longer, stirring occasionally. Remove bay leaf.

Arrange fish in greased shallow baking dish. Cover with vegetable mixture and bake at 400° for 30 minutes or until done. Serves six.

FAKED FROGLEGS

12 thighs from frying
  chicken
2 tbsp. pareve margarine
3 onions, chopped
3 creole tomatoes
1 sprig thyme
1 bay leaf
2 cloves garlic, minced

1 sweet pepper, chopped
  fine
¼ cup chopped mushrooms
½ cup tomato sauce
1 cup chicken consommé
dash Tabasco sauce
salt and pepper to taste

Brown thighs in margarine. After about 10 minutes add onion and brown with thighs. Add tomatoes; cover and let brown. Cook very slowly, adding salt and pepper to taste, Tabasco, thyme, bay leaf, and garlic.

Smother mixture slowly for 20 minutes, stirring frequently. Add sweet pepper, mushrooms, and tomato sauce and continue to cook slowly until thighs are tender.

Add chicken consommé and continue to cook slowly, covered, for about ½ hour. Serves four.

ACADIAN TROUT CASSEROLE

5 tbsp. butter
3 tbsp. flour
2 cups milk
2 tbsp. chopped shallots
½ cup chopped celery
1 tbsp. chopped parsley
1 tbsp. chopped green
   pepper
1 pimento, minced fine
2 tbsp. sherry

1 egg, well beaten
⅛ tsp. Tabasco sauce
1 tsp. salt
⅛ tsp. pepper
1 lb. smoked trout or carp,
   skinned, deboned, and
   flaked
¼ cup bread crumbs
1 tbsp. melted butter

Make a sauce with butter, flour, and milk. Stir in shallots, celery, parsley, green pepper, pimento, and sherry. Remove from heat. Add a small amount of hot mixture to egg and combine with remaining sauce. Add Tabasco sauce, salt, pepper, and flaked trout.

Place in 1½-quart casserole. Sprinkle top with bread crumbs that have been mixed with melted butter. Bake in 350-degree oven for 20 minutes. Serves six to eight.

CONGO SQUARE TOMATOES

8 large creole tomatoes
5 medium-size onions
4 cloves garlic
1 pinch thyme
1 bay leaf
½ lb. coarsely chopped
  kosher salami
1 tsp. salt

⅛ tsp. pepper
5 tbsp. melted schmaltz
½ tsp. oregano
2 tbsp. flour
bread crumbs

Cut off tops of tomatoes and remove pulp. Cook the pulp, four onions (chopped fine), and garlic, thyme, bay leaf, salt, pepper, and oregano for about 25 minutes. Add 3 tablespoons schmaltz mixed with flour. Cook for additional 20 minutes. Remove bay leaf.

Chop remaining onion fine; place in a separate pan with schmaltz and sauté. Add salami and cook for 10 minutes. Combine this mixture with seasoned tomato pulp. Stuff tomatoes and sprinkle tops with bread crumbs. Bake in 350-degree oven for 25 minutes. Serves eight.

BANDANA BANANAS

1 egg, beaten
½ cup sugar
1½ cup sifted flour
1 tsp. baking powder

¾ cup milk
2 ripe bananas
vegetable oil or butter for
  frying

Mash bananas. Mix well-beaten egg and milk together with dry ingredients. Add mixture to mashed bananas. Drop by the tablespoon in oil or butter and fry on a slow fire until golden brown. Turn and brown on other side. Makes about ten to fifteen fritters.

CREAMY PECAN PRALINES

1 cup brown sugar
½ cup light cream
1 cup pecan halves

1 cup white sugar
2 tbsp. butter

Dissolve sugars in cream and boil to the thread stage (228 degrees), stirring occasionally. Add butter and pecans. Cook until syrup reaches soft-ball stage (236 degrees). Cool; beat until somewhat thickened but not until it loses its gloss. Drop by the tablespoon onto a greased marble slab or double thickness of waxed paper. The candy will flatten out into large pieces. Makes twelve pralines.

EGGS ORLEANS

2½ cups tomatoes
½ green pepper, chopped
1 small onion, chopped
½ cup chopped celery
1 tsp. sugar
¾ tsp. salt

⅛ tsp. pepper
1 bay leaf
¾ cup bread crumbs
4 eggs
½ cup grated American
  cheese

Sauté tomatoes, peppers, onions, celery, sugar, salt, and pepper together for 10 minutes. Remove bay leaf, add bread crumbs, and place in casserole. Break eggs on top, sprinkle with salt and pepper, and cover with grated cheese. Bake at 350° until eggs are firm and cheese has melted (about 15 to 20 minutes). Serves four.

EGGS DE SUPERDOME

2 eggs, beaten
1 cup milk
1 cup sifted flour
4 hard-cooked eggs

1 tsp. baking powder
½ tsp. salt
⅓ cup butter

Heat greased casserole in oven. Beat eggs and milk thoroughly. Sift flour, baking powder, and salt together. Add milk and butter and beat mixture until smooth. Cover bottom of hot casserole with layer of eggs (halved, quartered, or sliced). Fill casserole about ⅔ full with batter and bake in 450-degree oven until mixture begins to expand and brown slightly. Reduce temperature to 350° and bake 25 minutes longer. Serve at once. Serves four.

STRUTTERS SPREAD

2 3¾-oz. cans salmon
1 avocado
1 tbsp. lemon juice
1 tbsp. olive or salad oil
1 clove garlic, finely
   chopped

1½ tsp. grated onion
½ tsp. salt
4 drops Tabasco sauce
crackers

Drain and flake salmon. Peel avocado, remove seed, and grate using a medium grater. Combine all ingredients and toss lightly. Serve with crackers. Makes about one pint.

DOUBLOON DIP

1 lb. smoked trout, skinned,
   deboned, and flaked
1 8-oz. package
   Philadelphia cream cheese

1 tsp. chopped chives
2 cups sour cream
½ stick butter

Melt cream cheese and butter until soft. Stir in flaked trout. Fold in sour cream. Add chives and salt to taste. Serve warm with assorted crackers or potato chips. Makes one pint.

PIANO ROLL POTATOES

6 baking potatoes (about
   3 lbs.), baked
¾ cup mayonnaise
3 tbsp. spicy brown mustard
1 small clove garlic, crushed
1 tsp. salt

¼ tsp. pepper
1 lb. kosher frankfurter,
   cooked and cut in diagonal
   slices

Cut potatoes in half. Scoop potato out (being careful not to damage skins) and mash. Add mayonnaise, mustard, garlic, salt, and pepper and mix well. Fold in frankfurter slices. Fill shells with large amounts of mixture and bake 20 minutes in 350-degree oven or until heated through. Serves four to six.

SWINGING RED BEAN SOUP

3 slices Beef Frye
1 onion, sliced thin
3 ribs celery, diced
2 bay leaves
1 tbsp. flour
2 cups hot water

2 cups cooked red beans
2 slices lemon
½ tsp. salt
pepper to taste
1 tbsp. Worcestershire
   sauce

Cook the Beef Frye, onion, and celery in a saucepan until onion is tender. Add bay leaves and flour and stir until smooth. Add hot water, red beans, lemon, salt, pepper, and Worcestershire sauce and cook for about 20 minutes.

Press through a coarse sieve and place back in saucepan. Heat thoroughly and serve. Serves four.

PASSOVER PAIN PERDU

½ cup milk
⅛ tsp. salt
2 eggs, well beaten
6 slices Passover sponge
   cake, cut in 1-inch
   slices

2 tbsp. butter
6 tbsp. sugar
1 tsp. cinnamon

Combine milk, salt, and eggs. Soak sponge cake slices in mixture. In skillet, fry in butter until well browned on both sides. Combine sugar and cinnamon and sprinkle over slices. Serve hot. Serves six.

SPRING FIESTA BAKED FLOUNDER

4 tsp. butter, divided
2 lbs. flounder filets
1 tsp. salt
½ tsp. hot-pepper sauce
1 tbsp. paprika

¼ cup grated cheddar
   cheese
1 cup dairy sour cream
¼ cup fine, dry bread
   crumbs

Grease a 2-quart baking dish with 1 tablespoon of butter. Arrange fish filets in baking dish. Blend salt, hot-pepper sauce, paprika, and cheddar cheese into sour cream and spread over fish. Top with bread crumbs and dot with remaining 3 teaspoons butter.

Bake uncovered at 350° for 30 minutes or until fish is easily flaked with fork. Serves four to six.

MAGNOLIA BLOSSOM PUDDING

3 eggs, slightly beaten
½ cup sugar
¾ tsp. salt
½ tsp. nutmeg
3 cups milk
¼ cup butter
1 cup cooked white rice

1 tsp. vanilla extract
⅓ cup pecan pieces
½ cup firmly packed brown
   sugar
½ tsp. rum extract
   (optional)

Combine eggs, sugar, salt, and nutmeg well. Heat milk and 2 tablespoons butter in a saucepan and scald. Pour into egg mixture slowly, stirring constantly.

Stir in rice, vanilla, and rum extract (if desired) and pour into a 1½-quart casserole. Place in a shallow pan of hot water. Bake at 350° for 30 minutes or until knife inserted in center comes out clean.

Remove pudding from oven and hot water. Brown pecans lightly in remaining butter and stir in brown sugar. Sprinkle over pudding. Broil about 3 inches from flame until hot and bubbly. Cool slightly. Pudding can be served warm or cold. Serves six to eight.

PECAN BRITTLE

2 cups sugar
1 cup broken pecans
⅛ tsp. salt

Melt sugar in heavy skillet over low heat, stirring constantly until consistency of a thin syrup (about 8 to 10 minutes). Add pecans and salt and stir until nuts are coated. Pour into a greased baking pan. When cold, break into small pieces. Makes one pound.

PICKLED GREEN PEPPERS

2 large green peppers
2 cloves garlic, cut up
¾ cup white vinegar

2 cups water
3 tsp. salt

Wash and slice green peppers into strips. Layer in jar with garlic. In separate bowl, combine vinegar, water, and salt. Mix well and pour over peppers. Marinate at least 36 hours at room temperature and then refrigerate. Serves four.

RIVER ROAD CORN RELISH

¼ cup sugar
½ cup tarragon vinegar
½ tsp. salt
¼ tsp. Tabasco sauce
½ tsp. celery seed
¼ tsp. mustard seed

2 cups cooked corn
2 tbsp. chopped green
  pepper
1 tbsp. chopped pimento
1 tbsp. minced onion

Combine sugar, vinegar, salt, Tabasco sauce, celery seed, and mustard seed in a saucepan. Bring to a boil and cook for 2 minutes. Remove from heat. Drain corn and add to vinegar mixture. Add remaining ingredients and mix. Place in a bowl, cover, and chill. Makes about two cups.

NONNIE'S CHOCOLATE ICEBOX PIE

1 12-oz. pkg. vanilla
 wafers
4 eggs, separated
½ lb. German chocolate

3 tbsp. water
3 tbsp. sugar
½ cup ground pecans

Melt chocolate in double boiler. Beat egg yolks until lemon colored. Add sugar and water to yolks and beat until well blended. Stir egg mixture into melted chocolate. Cook slowly in double boiler until mixture is thick and smooth (about consistency of custard), stirring constantly. Remove from heat. When cool, add stiffly beaten egg whites and pecans. Fold in until well blended. (Mixture will become thin.)

Line springform pan with vanilla wafers, then thin layer of chocolate filling; repeat, ending with chocolate filling. Place in refrigerator for 24 hours.

Remove sides of pan. Garnish with Topping (see recipe). (This recipe doubles easily to make an extra large pie; use the same size pan. Topping will remain the same for either size pie.)

Topping

½ pt. whipping cream
½ cup confectioners' sugar
½ tsp. vanilla extract

maraschino cherries and
 chopped pecans or pecan
 halves

Whip cream until thick. Blend in sugar and vanilla. Spread on top and sides of pie. Garnish with chopped pecans or pecan halves and cherries.

"NU-AW-LUNS" APPLE PIE

6 to 8 large apples
1 cup sugar
¼ tsp. salt
2 tsp. cinnamon

2 tbsp. flour
1 recipe 9-in. two-crust pie
    pastry
1 tbsp. pareve margarine

Pare and slice apples. Sift dry ingredients together and mix with apples. Line pan with pastry and fill with apple mixture. Dot with margarine and cover with lattice crust. Seal and flute edges. Bake at 450 degrees for 15 minutes. Lower temperature to 350° and continue baking 45 minutes longer. Remove from oven and cool on wire rack.

POISSON SAUCE

4 tbsp. butter
2 hard-cooked eggs, mashed
1 tbsp. capers
½ tbsp. creole mustard
½ tbsp. horseradish

1 tbsp. lemon juice
1 tbsp. Worcestershire
    sauce
1 clove garlic, minced
3 tbsp. white wine

Melt butter in saucepan on low flame. Add all other ingredients and mix well. Heat until hot. Pour over broiled fish fillets just before serving. Makes enough sauce for eight fish fillets.

GANG PLANK SALAD

2 cups smoked trout,
  skinned, deboned, and
  cut into 1-inch pieces
½ cup diced celery
½ cup mayonnaise

2 tbsp. capers
1 tbsp. lemon juice
1 tsp. salt
½ tsp. Tabasco sauce
4 large creole tomatoes

Toss trout pieces and celery together. Blend mayonnaise, capers, lemon juice, salt, and Tabasco sauce. Add ⅔ of this mixture to trout and celery, toss lightly.

Cut tomatoes into sixths, almost to the bottom, gently spreading sections apart. Fill tomatoes with trout mixture.

Place on bed of lettuce or salad gree ᴨ᷍ ꓤ top with remaining mayonnaise dressing. Serves four.

Glossary of Terms

Almondine: Prepared with almonds.

À la Creole: Cooked with the basic Creole ingredients of tomatoes, onions, and green peppers.

Au Gratin: With crumbs and/or grated cheese.

Baleboosteh: An excellent homemaker, or boss of the house.

Bamboula: An African dance.

Bayou: A marshy inlet or outlet of a lake, river, etc.; also a backwater.

Beef Frye: Kosher sliced cured smoked plate beef.

Beignets: French doughnuts sprinkled with powdered sugar.

Bisque: Thick soup usually made from shellfish.

Blintze: Thin pancake filled with cheese or fruit.

Boeuf Gras: "Fatted calf"; one of the symbols of Mardi Gras.

Bon Appétit: Means "I hope you enjoy your meal."

Bouillabaisse: A highly seasoned stew made of two or more kinds of fish and sometimes seasoned with wine.

Bouillon: A meat, chicken, or fish broth.

Braise: To brown meat or vegetables in very little hot fat, adding little liquid and cooking in covered vessel.

Café au Lait: Mixture of half strong coffee and half hot milk.

Café Brûlot: Coffee flavored with spices, flamed with brandy, and served from silver bowl.

Café Noir: Black coffee.

Café Royale: Black coffee served in demitasse, flavored with lump sugar soaked with brandy and ignited.

Cajun: A descendant of the Acadian French whose cooking is combined with Creole and Indian seasonings.

Calas: Rice cakes.

Calinda: An African dance.

Canapé: A toasted piece of bread or a cracker spread with a variety of meats, fish, cheese, etc.; served as an appetizer.

Carnival: Period of feasting and celebration before Lent, climaxed in New Orleans by Mardi Gras Day.

Chicory: A root, roasted and ground to flavor Louisiana coffee.

Courtbouillon: Fish stew made with tomato sauce.

Coush Coush: Variation of African and Acadian dish made with corn-meal mush.

Creole: Descendant of original French and Spanish settlers of Louisiana.

Creosher: A term created by the authors. A play upon combined words "Creole" and "Kosher."

Crepes: Thin pancakes.

Croûtons: Bread of various shapes (usually toasted), cut in small pieces.

En Brochette: A method of cooking meat or chicken livers on a skewer.

Étouffée: Smothered.

Faux Pas: A "no-no."

Filé: Powder made from dried sassafras leaves used to thicken gumbo.

Flambeaux: Flaming torches carried in Mardi Gras parades.

Frappé: Half frozen.

Fricassee: Dish made of poultry or meat stewed slowly in gravy.

Fritters: Small batter containing fruit or other ingredients, dropped into deep fat or sautéed.

Gallery: French for "porch."

Gefilte fish: A combination of various fish, chopped or ground; usually served as an appetizer.

Glacé: Glazed (meat is often glazed by being brushed with stock, sweets by being brushed with egg white or sugar syrup.)

Grillades: Square pieces of beef or veal browned, then simmered until tender in a brown tomato sauce.

Gris-gris: Charm, amulet, or potion believed to bring either luck or doom to individuals.

Grits: Coarsely ground hominy; indigenous to the South.

Gumbo: Highly seasoned thick soup made with okra and filé.

Hallah: Traditional braided egg bread.

Hors d'oeuvres: Various appetizers served before meals.

Jambalaya: Rice cooked with seafood, meat, or poultry.

Jazz: Music with syncopated rhythm.

Kashruth: Jewish dietary laws.

Kosher: Foods adhering to Jewish dietary laws.

Krewe: Carnival Club.

Kugel: Pudding.

Lagniappe: Something extra; small gift of appreciation.

Latkes: Potato pancakes.

L'Chaim: Means "to life"; an expression used to toast an occasion.

Levee: Embankment for preventing flooding of rivers.

Lox: Smoked salmon.

Mardi Gras: French for "Fat Tuesday." Day of feasting before first day of Lent.

Marinate: To let stand in seasoned liquid or paste for varying lengths of time.

Matzo meal: Substitute for bread or cracker crumbs used mainly during Passover.

Mirliton: Pear-shaped vegetable in squash family, sometimes called "vegetable pear."

Noshe: A "snack."

Nosher: One who likes to snack or sample food.

Pain perdu (lost bread): Variety of French Toast.

Pareve: Foods that may be served with either milk or meat dishes.

Passover: Eight-day Jewish holiday commemorating freedom from slavery.

Pâté: Pastry shell with meat, fish, vegetable, or sweet filling; also a meat paste.

Pesach: Jewish and Hebrew word for Passover.

Piquant: Sharp, spicy flavor.

Pirogue: Canoe made by hollowing out a large log.

Plantain: Member of banana family which requires cooking.

Porte Cochère: Carriage entrance.

Potpourri: Miscellaneous collection.

Poulet: French for chicken.

Praline: Creole candy made from pecans and sugar.

Purée: Food finely blended or mashed.

Red beans: Kidney beans.

Remoulade: Sauce of spices and seasonings used over seafood.

Rex: "King" of Mardi Gras.

Roux: Basic mixture of flour and shortening used for thickening sauces, gravies, and soups.

Sauté: To fry lightly in very little fat.

Schmaltz: Rendered chicken fat.

Shallots: A plant of the onion kind whose bulb is used for flavoring; same as green onions.

Soirées: Creole expression for "evening at home."

Soufflé: Any of several baked foods made light and puffy by addition of beaten eggs before baking. Served as main course or sweetened as a dessert.

Voodoo: Mysterious rites practiced by Louisiana slaves and early white settlers.

Yams: Southern sweet potatoes.

Yom Tov: "Good day"; greeting used on Jewish holidays, or an expresson referring to holiday itself.

Index

KOSHER CREOLE COOKBOOK   **213**

SOUFFLÉS (*See* Eggs)

SOUPS

VEAL

VEGETABLES

Notes

Notes

Notes

Notes

Notes

Notes

KOSHER CREOLE COOKBOOK

Please send me _____ copies of **Kosher Creole Cookbook** at $8.95
each. Enclosed please find my check in the amount of _____ to
cover cost of book, including 85¢ postage and handling for one copy; 25¢
for each additional copy ordered. (Louisiana residents add applicable sales
tax.)

Name _____

Address _____

City/State _____ Zip Code _____

Pelican Publishing Co., P.O. Box 189, Gretna, LA 70053

KOSHER CREOLE COOKBOOK

Please send me _____ copies of **Kosher Creole Cookbook** at $8.95
each. Enclosed please find my check in the amount of _____ to
cover cost of book, including 85¢ postage and handling for one copy; 25¢
for each additional copy ordered. (Louisiana residents add applicable sales
tax.)

Name _____

Address _____

City/State _____ Zip Code _____

Pelican Publishing Co., P.O. Box 189, Gretna, LA 70053

KOSHER CREOLE COOKBOOK

Please send me _____ copies of **Kosher Creole Cookbook** at $8.95
each. Enclosed please find my check in the amount of _____ to
cover cost of book, including 85¢ postage and handling for one copy; 25¢
for each additional copy ordered. (Louisiana residents add applicable sales
tax.)

Name _____

Address _____

City/State _____ Zip Code _____

Pelican Publishing Co., P.O. Box 189, Gretna, LA 70053